MW01255826

FLORIDA LAW ENFORCEMENT
BASIC ABILITIES TEST (BAT)
EXAM GUIDE

Prepare for Success!

Angelo Tropea

Copyright 2016 by Angelo Tropea. All rights reserved. No part of this book may be reproduced in any form or by any electronic or mechanical means, including information storage and retrieval systems without permission in writing from the publisher, except by a reviewer, who may quote brief passages in a review. Any similarity of names of persons, addresses, places and telephone numbers used in this book to any actual names of persons, addresses and telephone numbers is purely coincidental.

ISBN-13: 978-1540506122
ISBN-10: 1540506126

Published by Angelo Tropea Books Inc.

Please note that the passages, examples and questions used in this book are for study purposes only and do not reflect official names, codes, policies, rules or procedures of any governmental or public or private business, agency or department.

Unless otherwise clearly indicated, any similarity of names of persons, addresses, places and telephone numbers used in this book to any actual names of persons, addresses and telephone numbers is purely coincidental.

The information and web addresses presented in this book are current as of November 2016, but may change as time passes. Always consult the official Florida BAT site and other official sites for the most up-to-date information.

CONTENTS

HOW TO PREPARE FOR SUCCESS   1

There are probably as many ways to study successfully as there are people. However, in more than thirty years of preparing study materials and conducting classes for civil service exams, I have found that certain methods seem to work better than others with the great majority of students. The following are time-tested suggestions that you might want to consider as you incorporate this book in the study plan that is best for you.

SUGGESTIONS

1. Read carefully any current announcements by Florida governmental or official agencies relating to exams for law enforcement positions. Please note that there are presently three companies that administer the BAT test (Florida **B**asic **A**bilities **T**est).

2. Become familiar with the "BAT" test. It is the first step in entering a basic recruit training program for law enforcement or corrections. (See the web pages below for full information.)

The multiple-choice tests (2-2½ hours) have been developed by three officially designated providers and are administered by them either by way of regular paper format or a computer terminal. The three tests differ slightly in content and the passing grade for each test also varies.

Full information on the Florida BAT test is available at:

http://www.fdle.state.fl.us/cms/CJSTC/Officer-Requirements/Basic-Abilities-Test.aspx

Information about the approved vendors and the approved tests (Law Enforcement and Correctional) is available at:

http://www.fdle.state.fl.us/cms/CJSTC/Officer-Requirements/Providers.aspx

- The BAT is administered in the state of Florida.
- The passing scores are valid for four years from the date of the test.

The areas tested by the BAT are the following:

(Note: Check each provider website to learn which of the following subject areas are included in their test).

- written comprehension
- written expression
- information ordering

- spatial orientation
- memorization
- problem sensitivity
- inductive reasoning
- deductive reasoning
- selective attention
- flexibility of closure

3. Skim the contents of this book by reading the table of contents and then looking at each section to see the different types of questions and how they correspond to the official on-line descriptions of the BAT (**B**asic **A**bilities **T**est) for each of the three vendors.

4. Try to study every day for at least half an hour – and longer (1-2 hours) if you can. To get the greatest benefit, try not to have very long sessions. Studies have indicated that frequent shorter sessions are more effective than fewer, longer ones.

5. Study in a quiet, well-lit area with as few distractions as possible. This will help you to obtain the maximum benefit from each session.

6. Work on sections 3 – 13 in this book. They will introduce you to each type of question and provide practice questions with the answers explained.

Do not continue to the practice test until you have mastered all the different types of questions. Read all the comments after each answer to reinforce important facts and test-answering techniques. Try to record your answers on a separate sheet of paper and not in the book. This will make it easier for you to come back to the questions and answer them again without being influenced by your prior work.

7. Now tackle the multiple-choice Practice Exam. The exam has 100 questions, close to what you may see on the actual BAT (100-125 questions). Pay careful attention to every question that you don't answer correctly. If necessary, review the section in the book that relates to that type of question.

Try to take the practice exam in a single session (about 2 hours). By doing so, you will gain a valuable understanding of how long your attention span must last during the actual exam.

8. Because the test is administered on the computer, make sure that <u>before</u> the test date you're familiar with the computer keyboard and the fundamentals of computer operation.

At the test site, listen carefully to the directions on how to use the computer, including how to select or change answers. Also, listen carefully to the procedure to follow if there is a computer malfunction. If you're not certain about anything, ask questions.

9. If some questions are hard for you, keep in mind what Thomas Edison once said: "Genius is one percent inspiration and ninety-nine percent perspiration."

The aim of this book is to keep it **<u>simple</u> and <u>focused</u>** on the written exam, instead of complicating it with other information about police officer jobs, tests and benefits in other cities and states which does <u>NOT</u> contribute to attaining a higher score.

This book provides **exercises, explanations, and hints** about the types of questions that may be asked on the test with the aim of maximizing your score and thereby increasing your chances of being considered for a job.

Therefore, study every day.

Take this book with you – and make it your friend.

"That which we persist in doing becomes easier, not that the task itself has become easier, but that our ability to perform it has improved."

- Ralph Waldo Emerson

TYPES OF QUESTIONS ON TEST	
Section	**Question Type**
3	**Written Comprehension** questions evaluate a candidate's ability to understand written passages, especially details in sentences and paragraphs. On the job, you may apply this skill to understand policies, procedures, legal material and the laws of Florida.
4	**Written Expression** questions evaluate a candidate's ability to express herself clearly in written form. This skill is important in writing such things as memos, affidavits, and incident reports.
5	**Memorization** questions evaluate a candidate's ability to remember information that is provided in the form of pictures, numbers, procedures, etc. Remembering the details of the scene of a crime and remembering instructions are very important for a police officer.
6	**Problem Sensitivity** questions evaluate a candidate's ability to see the elements of a problem and the problem in its entirety. This skill is important because realizing that a situation might go wrong may help to prevent it.
7	**Deductive Reasoning** questions evaluate a candidate's ability to understand general rules and apply them to specific situations. This skill is useful when reading laws or regulations and applying them to actual situations.
8	**Inductive Reasoning** questions evaluate a candidate's ability to combine details or separate pieces of information to form general rules. This skill is important when assembling separate pieces of evidence or clues to determine what occurred and whether any laws are violated.

Section	Question Type
9	**Information Ordering** questions evaluate a candidate's ability to put in order given rules or actions. The rules or actions can include letters, words, sentences, procedures, pictures, and logical or mathematical operations. This skill is useful in such matters as following rules, issuing documents, and making arrests.
10	**Spatial Orientation** questions evaluate a candidate's ability to determine the candidate's location and the location of an object with respect to the candidate. This is important in understanding your location with respect to another location to which you must travel, as in an emergency response.
11	**Visualization** questions evaluate a candidate's ability to understand how an object would look when it is rotated or unfolded, or moved in any manner. Questions may also evaluate a candidate's skill in combining details or individual pieces of a two-dimensional or physical object to visualize the entire object.
12	**Flexibility of Closure** questions test a candidate's ability to locate something (an object, shape, etc.) that is difficult to see because it is mixed with a group of other objects or shapes or letters, etc.
13	**Selective Attention** questions test your ability to concentrate on a task without being distracted by things around you or around what you are concentrating on. This skill is important when trying to remember license plate numbers or other numeric or letter information.

Note: Please check with each test provider website to learn which of the subject areas are included on their test.

WRITTEN COMPREHENSION

3

These questions evaluate your ability to understand written passages, especially **details** in sentences and paragraphs.

A written passage is presented and questions are asked that require you to carefully refer back to the passage.

SUGGESTIONS

Read all four choices (A, B, C, and D) and carefully consider each one before deciding which choice is best.

Pay careful attention to the details. Match every detail of each choice to the detail in the passage.

The correct answer will be the choice that most nearly matches all the details.

(To double-check your answer, make sure that the other choices are not correct because they contain at least one detail that does not match what is stated in the passage.)

Questions 1 – 3

Answer questions 1 - 3 based on the information contained in the following paragraphs.

Police Officers Juan Medina and Cheryl Johnston were on foot patrol on July 4, 2016 when at 10:15 a.m. they came upon the scene of a minor traffic accident (at 5th Avenue and 48th Street) that had occurred 5 minutes earlier. Officer Medina called the Police Dispatcher at 10:20 a.m. and reported that the two drivers, who were the only persons in the vehicles, did not sustain any personal injuries. One of the vehicles, the one driven by a male named William Buxton, did have minor damage to the front bumper, and the other vehicle, driven by a male named Jack Solmer, had extensive damage to the rear bumper.

Officer Juan Medina examined the driver's licenses, vehicle registration certificates and vehicle insurance identification cards. The auto driven by William Buxton, age 39, was a silver 2009 Lexus, FL. license plate 9327ZA, owned by the driver, residing at 2932 East 78th Street, Miami, FL. Mr. Buxton's Florida driver's license identification number is D1749 38647 92132 and the expiration date is November 30, 2018.

The driver of the other auto was Jack Solmer, age 41, residing at 9822 East 7th Street, Miami, FL. Mr. Solmer's auto was a blue 2007 Infinity, FL. license plate 407PMB. Mr. Solmer's driver's license identification number is A214 295 337 and the expiration date is December 31, 2018.

Officers Medina and Johnston completed a Vehicle Accident Report at 10:35 a.m. The report number was 08492647437.

-----

1. Select the best answer: What is the time of the accident?
A. 10:15 a.m.   C. 10:20 a.m.
B. 10:35 a.m.   D. before 10:15 a.m.

----

2. How many persons were injured because of the traffic accident?
A. 1   C. 2
B. 0   D. none of the above

----

3. Which car sustained extensive damage to the rear bumper?
A. FL. plate #407PMB, silver 2007 Infinity
B. FL. plate #9327ZA, silver 2009 Lexus
C. FL. plate #9327ZA, blue 2009 Lexus
D. FL. plate #407PMB, blue 2007 Infinity

<u>Answers 1 – 3</u>
(Correct answers are in **<u>bold and underlined</u>**.)

1. Select the best answer: What is the time of the accident?
A. 10:15 a.m.   C. 10:20 a.m.
B. 10:35 a.m.   **<u>D. before 10:15 a.m.</u>**

("Police Officers Juan Medina and Cheryl Johnston were on foot patrol on July 4, 2016 when at 10:15 a.m. they came upon the scene of a minor traffic accident (at 5th Avenue and 48th Street, Miami, FL.) that had occurred <u>5 minutes earlier</u>."

The traffic accident happened 5 minutes <u>before</u> 10:15 a.m. (the time that the officers arrived at the scene). Therefore, the accident happened at 10:10 a.m. This 10:10 a.m. time is not listed as one of the choices, and choices "B" and "C" are times <u>after</u> 10:15 a.m. The best choice therefore is **"<u>D. before 10:15 a.m.</u>"**)

----

2. How many persons were injured because of the traffic accident?
A. 1   C. 2
<u>B. 0</u>   D. none of the above

(In paragraph one it states, "... the two drivers, who were the only persons in the vehicles, did <u>not</u> sustain any personal injuries.")

----

3. Which car sustained extensive damage to the rear bumper?
A. FL. plate #407PMB, silver 2007 Infinity
B. FL. plate #9327ZA, silver 2009 Lexus
C. FL. plate #9327ZA, blue 2009 Lexus
<u>D. FL. plate #407PMB, blue 2007 Infinity</u>

(In paragraph one it states, **"…**the other vehicle, driven by a male named Jack Solmer, had extensive damage to the rear bumper…." In paragraph three it states, Mr. Solmer's auto was a <u>blue 2007 Infinity, FL. license plate 407PMB</u>." The answer is choice "<u>D</u>" and not choice "A" because in choice "A" the color of the vehicle is stated as silver.)

Questions 4 - 6

Answer questions 4 - 6 based on the information contained in the following paragraphs.

Police Officers Jonathan Spencer and Anita Korich were on patrol in their squad car on May 17, 2016 when at 4:47 p.m. they witnessed a traffic accident at the intersection of 13th Avenue and 39th Street in Atlantic Beach. Officer Spencer called the Police Dispatcher at 4:55 p.m. and reported that the two drivers and their six passengers (three in each vehicle) did not sustain any personal injuries. One of the vehicles, the one driven by a male, Clark Winston, had damage to the driver's door, and the other vehicle, driven by a female, Beverly Marino, had damage to the front bumper and right side.

Officer Korich examined the driver's licenses, vehicle registration certificates and vehicle insurance identification cards. The auto driven by Clark Winston, age 49, was a red 2010 Ford Fusion, FL. license plate 3374BH, owned by the driver, residing at 2532 Cadman Plaza, Atlantic Beach, FL. Mr. Winston's Florida driver's license identification number is M3842 48547 62537 and the expiration date is October 31, 2018.

The driver of the other auto was Beverly Marino, age 54, residing at 165 Kings Avenue, Atlantic Beach, FL. Ms. Marino's auto was a black 2008 Ford Taurus, FL. license plate 5491HKD. Ms. Marino's driver's license identification number is B315 396 236 and the expiration is December 31, 2018.

Officers Spencer and Korich completed a Vehicle Accident Report at 5:35 p.m. The report number was 04495642441.

-----

4. What is the time of the accident?
A. 4:47 a.m.   C. 5:35 p.m.
B. 5:55 p.m.   D. 4:47 p.m.

----

5. Which car sustained damage to the front bumper and right side?
A. FL. plate #5497HDK, black 2008 Ford Taurus
B. FL. plate #3374BH, red 2010 Ford Fusion
C. FL. plate #5491HKD, black 2008 Ford Taurus
D. FL. plate #3374BH, red 2001 Ford Fusion

----

6. What is the total number of persons in the two vehicles?
A. 2   C. 9
B. 6   D. none of

Answers 4 - 6
(Correct answers are in **bold and underlined**.)

4. What is the time of the accident?
A. 4:47 a.m.
B. 5:55 p.m.
C. 5:35 p.m.
D. 4:47 p.m.

(In paragraph one it states, "Police Officers Jonathan Spencer and Anita Korich were on patrol in their squad car on May 17, 2016 when at 4:47 p.m. they witnessed a traffic accident....")

----

5. Which car sustained damage to the front bumper and right side?
A.   FL. plate #5497HDK, black 2008 Ford Taurus
B.   FL. plate #3374BH, red 2010 Ford Fusion
C.   FL. plate #5491HKD, black 2008 Ford Taurus
D.   FL. plate #3374BH, red 2001 Ford Fusion

(In paragraph one it states, "...the other vehicle, driven by a female, Beverly Marino, had damage to the front bumper and right side." Paragraph three states, "Ms. Marino's auto was a black 2008 Ford Taurus, FL. license plate 5491HKD.")

----

6. What is the total number of persons in the two vehicles?
A. 2
B. 6
C. 9
D. none of the above

(In paragraph one it states, "...the two drivers and their six passengers did not sustain any personal injuries."
(2 drivers + 6 passengers = 8 persons)
The correct answer (8) is not listed as a choice. Therefore, **"D. none of the above,"** is the correct choice.)

FLORIDA LAW ENFORCEMENT BASIC ABILITIES TEST (BAT) EXAM GUIDE

Questions 7 - 10

Answer questions 7 - 10 based on the information contained in the following paragraphs.

Police Officers Albert Dixon and Susan Chin were on patrol in their squad car on June 7, 2016 when at 6:35 p.m. a man approached them. The man pointed to his parked car and stated that a blue Infinity had just sideswiped it. The blue Infinity was now stopped about one hundred feet down the block. Police Officer Albert Dixon called the police dispatcher at 6:40 p.m. and reported the traffic accident (which occurred in front of 745 3rd Avenue, Boca Raton). Police Officer Susan Chin questioned the driver of the stopped blue Infinity. Both Police Officers reported to the dispatcher that the driver of the blue Infinity and the owner of the sideswiped car (a 2008 Chevy Malibu) did not sustain any injuries. Also, there were no passengers in the two cars. One of the vehicles, the blue Infinity, was driven and owned by a male, Matthew Fowler. It had damage to the front bumper. The other vehicle, owned by a male, Mark Peterson, had damage to the two doors on the driver's side.

Officer Dixon examined the driver's licenses, vehicle registration certificates and vehicle insurance identification cards. The auto driven by Matthew Fowler, age 42, was a blue 2012 Infinity, FL. license plate 45834DK, owned by the driver, residing at 147-49 Ferdinand Road, Boca Raton, FL. Mr. Fowler's Florida driver's license identification number is P3647 38537 22438 and the expiration date is September 30, 2018.

The owner of the parked auto was Mark Peterson, age 57, residing at 284 West 6th Street, Boca Raton, FL. Mr. Peterson's auto was a silver 2008 Chevy Malibu, Florida license plate 2493GKL. Mr. Peterson's driver's license identification number is C615 792 339 and the expiration is November 30, 2018.

Officers Dixon and Chin completed a Vehicle Accident Report at 7:05 p.m. The report number was 024976454324.

-----

7. Select the best answer: The time of the accident is approximately:
A. 6:35 a.m.   C. 9:40 p.m.
B. 6:53 p.m.   D. 6:35 p.m.

----

8. Which car sustained damage to the two doors on the driver's side?
A.   FL. plate #45834DK, blue 2012 Infinity
B.   FL. plate #2493GKL, silver 2008 Chevy Malibu
C.   FL. plate #45834DK, silver 2012 Infinity
D.   FL. plate #2493GKL, blue 2008 Chevy Malibu

9. What is the total number of persons (drivers or owners) involved?
A. 1
B. 2
C. 3
D. none of the above

----

10. The owner of the parked vehicle resides at:
A. 284 West 6th Street, Miami, FL.
B. 745 3rd Avenue, Boca Raton, FL.
C. 147-49 Ferdinand Road, Boca Raton, FL.
D. 284 West 6th Street, Boca Raton, FL.

Answers 7 – 10
(Correct answers are in **bold and underlined**.)

7. Select the best answer: The time of the accident is approximately:
A. 6:35 a.m.
B. 6:53 p.m.
C. 9:40 p.m.
D. 6:35 p.m.

(In paragraph one it states, "Police Officers Albert Dixon and Susan Chin were on patrol in their squad car on June 7, 2016 when at <u>6:35 p.m.</u> a man approached them. The man pointed to his parked car and stated that a blue Infinity had <u>just</u> sideswiped it.")

----

8. Which car sustained damage to the two doors on the driver's side?
A.   FL. plate #45834DK, blue 2012 Infinity
B.   FL. plate #2493GKL, silver 2008 Chevy Malibu
C.   FL. plate #45834DK, silver 2012 Infinity
D.   FL. plate #2493GKL, blue 2008 Chevy Malibu

(In paragraph two it states, "The owner of the parked auto was Mark Peterson, age 57, residing at 284 West 6th Street, Boca Raton, FL. Mr. Peterson's auto was a <u>silver 2008 Chevy Malibu, FL. license plate 2493GKL</u>.")

----

9. What is the total number of persons (drivers or owners) involved?
A. 1
B. 2
C. 3
D. none of the above

(Only the two drivers were involved. "Both Police Officers reported to the dispatcher that the driver of the blue Infinity and the owner of the sideswiped car (a 2008 Chevy Malibu) did not sustain any injuries. Also, "...there were no passengers in the two cars.")

----

10. The owner of the parked vehicle resides at:
A. 284 West 6th Street, Miami, FL.
B. 745 3rd Avenue, Boca Raton, FL.
C. 147-49 Ferdinand Road, Boca Raton, FL.
D. 284 West 6th Street, Boca Raton, FL.

(Paragraph 3: "The owner of the parked auto was Mark Peterson, age 57, residing at 284 West 6th Street, Boca Raton, FL.")

_____

> "Practice even the things you despair in, for even the left hand, ineffectual for things for want of practice, holds the bridle more vigorously than the right hand; for it has been practiced in this."
>
> - Marcus Aurelius

WRITTEN EXPRESSION

4

These questions evaluate your ability to express yourself clearly enough so that others will understand.

Two or more versions of a written sample are provided.

You are asked to decide which version(s) are clear, accurate, complete, and grammatically correct.

In deciding which versions are correct, consider the following (one at a time):

Is the **grammar <u>correct</u>**?

Is the **passage <u>clear</u>**?

Is the **information <u>accurate</u>**?

Is the **information <u>complete</u>**?

Before we answer practice questions, let's discuss an approach to this type of question and do a quick review of some basic rules of grammar, usage, punctuation and sentence structure.

FIRST, READ EACH SENTENCE CAREFULLY TO SEE IF IT HAS ANY OF THE FOLLOWING FLAWS:

1. DOES IT SOUND LIKE ENGLISH - OR DOES IT SOUND LIKE STREET TALK?
Some obvious examples: (Underlining is for emphasis of correct/incorrect English usage.)
    Correct: I <u>go</u> to the store every day.
    Not Correct: I <u>goes</u> to the store every day.

    Correct: It <u>doesn't</u> matter how much it costs.
    Not Correct: It <u>don't</u> matter how much it costs.

2. IS THE SENTENCE IN A LOGICAL ORDER? ARE THE MAIN IDEAS PROPERLY CONNECTED?
Example: Which of the following three choices is/are correct?
    (1) The boy who dropped out of high school didn't like to study.
    (2) The boy didn't like to study dropped out of high school.
    (3) The boy dropped out didn't like to study.
Answer: (1) is the most logical and grammatically correct.

3. ARE THERE ANY MISSPELLED WORDS?
Example:
    assistant and NOT asistant
    court facility and NOT court fasility
    believe and NOT beleive
    precinct and NOT precint

4. ARE WORDS USED CORRECTLY?
    The principal (NOT principle) of the school was Mr. Kane.
    The advice (NOT advise) was very welcomed.
    They complimented (NOT complemented) her for her hard work.
    Their (NOT there) car needed repair.
    He picked up the stationery (NOT stationary) for the captain in room 605.
    He was too (NOT "to" or "two") happy to speak.
    The Police Officer accepted (NOT excepted) the medal.
    The work site (NOT cite) was very clean.
    Someone who is not moving is stationary (NOT stationery).
    The capital city (NOT capitol) of Florida State is Tallahassee.

5. ARE APOSTROPHES USED CORRECTLY?
    The boy's (NOT boys) hat was yellow.

If you cannot eliminate the sentence as being bad after applying the preceding general rules, review the sentence for the following grammatical errors. (Remember that for all the following general rules, there are exceptions.)

1. EVERY SENTENCE BEGINS WITH A CAPITAL LETTER AND ENDS WITH A PERIOD.

2. FOR A SENTENCE TO BE COMPLETE, IT MUST HAVE AT MINIMUM A SUBJECT AND A PREDICATE. OTHERWISE, IT IS JUST A SENTENCE FRAGMENT.

A **subject** is usually a noun about which something is asked or stated.
Example: The police officer (subject) speaks softly.

A **predicate** contains a verb and is the part of the sentence about what is said about the subject. In the above example, the predicate is "speaks."

3. A VERB AND ITS SUBJECT MUST AGREE IN NUMBER.
The police officers <u>looks</u> tall. (NOT CORRECT because "police officers" is plural.)
The police officers <u>look</u> tall. (CORRECT because "look" is used with a plural subject.)

Police officers are <u>plural</u> (more than one). "Police officers" and "look" agree in number.

Another example:
The men and the woman <u>works</u> in the same precinct. (NOT CORRECT)
The men and the woman <u>work</u> in the same precinct. (CORRECT)

The men and the woman is a plural subject and takes a plural verb <u>work</u>.

The boy <u>works</u> (singular verb). The boy and girl <u>work</u> (plural verb).

4. A COMMA USUALLY GOES BEFORE THE FOLLOWING WORDS - but, for, or, nor, so, yet - WHEN THE WORD CONNECTS TWO MAIN CLAUSES.
Examples:
He didn't like to study, but he liked to play.
He scored a high mark, for he had received good training.
You can try hard and succeed, or you can make a feeble attempt and fail.
He didn't try hard, nor did he try for long.
He studied long and hard, so he passed.
He was sick when he took the test, yet he did very well.

5. A COMMA USUALLY GOES AFTER AN INTRODUCTORY PHRASE.
Examples:
When you study, you build up the neural connections in your brain.
Because of hard work and a little good luck, he succeeded in life.

6. A COMMA USUALLY GOES BETWEEN SEPARATE ITEMS IN A LIST OR SERIES OF ADJECTIVES.
Examples:
The boy was young, proud, and happy.

The tall, young, proud boy walked up to the front of the room.

7. COMMAS USUALLY SET OFF <u>PARENTHETICAL ELEMENTS</u>.
Examples:
Young boys, <u>as Abraham Lincoln once observed</u>, should not be afraid to work hard.
American soldiers, <u>generally speaking,</u> are very well trained.

8. A SEMICOLON IS USUALLY USED BETWEEN MAIN CLAUSES NOT LINKED BY and, but, for, or, nor, so, yet.
Examples:
The young boys played basketball; the older men sat on the bleachers.
The war had many battles; few were as fierce as this one.

Notice that the letter after the semicolon is NOT capitalized.

9. THE COLON IS USUALLY USED TO DIRECT ATTENTION TO A SERIES (A LIST).
Example: The ingredients of success are as follows: hard work, commitment, and luck.

If grammar is not your strong point, or if you feel you need to concentrate more on it, there are many "rules of grammar" books available. For free online resources, search "rules of grammar" for an almost endless number of informative websites.

Question 1

1. An officer is reviewing a report she is preparing. It contains the following two rough drafts. Which of the two sentences are grammatically correct?

   1. Proper training and attitude proper grooming and proper wearing of a well maintained uniform are important in conveying a confident and professional appearance

   2. In addition to proper training and attitude, proper grooming and the wearing of a well maintained uniform are important in conveying a confident and professional appearance.

A. Only sentence 1 is grammatically correct.
B. Only sentence 2 is grammatically correct.
C. Both sentences 1 and 2 are grammatically correct.
D. Neither sentence 1 nor sentence 2 is grammatically correct.

Answer 1

ANSWER IS "B. Only sentence 2 is grammatically correct."
(Sentence 1 needs a comma after "attitude" and a period at the end of the sentence.)

Applicable rules:
"A comma usually goes between separate items on a list or series of adjectives."
"Every sentence begins with a capital letter and ends with a period."

Questions 2 – 3

2. An officer is asked by his partner to review a report that the partner is preparing. It contains the following two versions of one part of the report. Which are grammatically correct?

    1. Mr Jones stated that although he would accept the speeding ticket, he would not pay it on principal and that he would immediately tear it up.

    2. Mr Jones said that he would accept the speeding ticket, but on principle he would not pay it and would immediately tear it up.

A. Only sentence 1 is grammatically correct.
B. Only sentence 2 is grammatically correct.
C. Both sentences 1 and 2 are grammatically correct.
D. Neither sentence 1 nor sentence 2 is grammatically correct.

----

3. An officer is preparing a report and has not decided which of two versions of a specific section he wishes to use. Which of the following two versions are grammatically correct?

    1. Mr. Kim Jones and Mr. David Alsbury has not decided whether to testify. Both believe that the complaint is not merited.

    2. Mr. Kim Jones and Mr. David Alsbury have not decided whether to testify. Both beleive that the complaint is not merited.

A. Only sentence 1 is grammatically correct.
B. Only sentence 2 is grammatically correct.
C. Both sentences 1 and 2 are grammatically correct.
D. Neither sentence 1 nor sentence 2 is grammatically correct.

Answers 2 – 3

2. An officer is asked by his partner to review a report that the officer is preparing. It contains the following two versions of one part of the report. Which are grammatically correct?

    1. <u>Mr</u> Jones stated that although he would accept the speeding ticket, he would not pay it on <u>principal</u> and that he would immediately tear it up.

    2. <u>Mr</u> Jones said that he would accept the speeding ticket, but on principle he would

not pay it and would immediately tear it up.

D. Neither sentence 1 nor sentence 2 is grammatically correct.
(Both sentences need a period at the end of "Mr." Also, "principal" in sentence 1 should be "principle.")

----

3. An officer is preparing a report and has not decided which of two versions of a specific section he wishes to use. Which of the following two versions are grammatically correct?

   1. Mr. Kim Jones and Mr. David Alsbury <u>has</u> not decided whether to testify. Both believe that the complaint is not merited.

   2. Mr. Kim Jones and Mr. David Alsbury have not decided whether to testify. Both <u>beleive</u> that the complaint is not merited.

D. Neither sentence 1 nor sentence 2 is grammatically correct.
(The "has" in sentence 1 should be "have" and "beleive" in sentence two should be "believe.")

Questions 4 - 6

4. Police Officer Charles Pinto is preparing a speech that he will give at a community meeting. Which of the following two versions are correct?

   1. Persons should call 911 to report emergencies they will receive a fast response.

   2. Persons should call 911 to report emergencies. They will receive a fast response.

A. 1 only is correct.

B. 2 only is correct.

C. Neither 1 nor 2 is correct.

D. Both 1 and 2 are correct

----

5. Police Officer Janet Ryker is preparing an instruction sheet on how to process reports. Which of the following two versions are correct?

   1. Properly preparing reports is an important part of a Police Officers duties. This is especially true when filling out reports of aided cases or unusual occurrences.

   2. Properly preparing reports is an important part of a Police Officer's duties this is especially true when filling out reports of aided cases or unusual occurrences.

A. 1 only is correct.

B. 2 only is correct.

C. Neither 1 nor 2 is correct.

D. Both 1 and 2 are correct.

----

6. Police Officer Kim Gallon is checking the correctness of sentences in one of her reports. Which of the following two sentences are correct?

    1. Because rules and reggulations must be clearly understood and correctly applied, your ability to understand and apply facts and information to given situations is vital for the proper performance of your duties.

    2. Because rules and regulations must be clearly understood and correctly applied, your ability to understand and apply facts and information to given situations is vital for the proper performence of your duties.

A. 1 only is correct.   C. Neither 1 nor 2 is correct.

B. 2 only is correct.   D. Both 1 and 2 are correct.

Answers 4 – 6

4. Police Officer Charles Pinto is preparing a speech that he will give at a local community meeting. Which of the following two sentences are correct?

    1. Persons should call 911 to report <u>emergencies they</u> will receive a fast response.

    2. Persons should call 911 to report emergencies. They will receive a fast response.

B. 2 only is correct.

(Sentence one is a run-on sentence. It needs a period after "emergencies" and a capital "T" for the word "they.")

----

5. Police Officer Janet Ryker is preparing an instruction sheet on how to process reports. Which of the following two versions are correct?

    1. Properly preparing reports is an important part of a <u>Police Officers</u> duties. This is especially true when filling out reports of aided cases or unusual occurrences.

2. Properly preparing reports is an important part of a Police Officer's <u>duties this</u> is especially true when filling out reports of aided cases or unusual occurrences.

C. Neither 1 nor 2 is correct.

(One is not correct because "a Police Officers" should be "a Police Officer's" – <u>singular possessive</u>. Two is not correct because it is a run-on sentence. It should have a period after "duties" and a capital "T" for the word "this.")

6. Police Officer Kim Gallon is checking the correctness of sentences in one of her reports. Which of the following two sentences are correct?

1. Because rules and <u>reggulations</u> must be clearly understood and correctly applied, your ability to understand and apply facts and information to given situations is vital for the proper performance of your duties.

2. Because rules and regulations must be clearly understood and correctly applied, your ability to understand and apply facts and information to given situations is vital for the proper <u>performence</u> of your duties.

C. Neither 1 nor 2 is correct.

(One is not correct because the word "regulations" is misspelled "reggulations." Two is not correct because the word "performance" is misspelled "performence.")

Another type of WRITTEN EXPRESSION question may ask you to select the best summary of the information that is provided.

The best summary is the one that expresses the information in the most <u>clear, accurate and complete manner.</u>

Before we try to answer a question of this type, let's consider the following simple example:

> ### Information provided:
> A 16 year old boy was struck by a 2002 Buick on August 17, 2016.

Not clear:

2002 Buick on August 17, 2016, a 16 year old boy.

Clear:

A 2002 Buick, on August 17, 2016, struck a 16 year old boy.

Not accurate:

A 16 year old boy was struck by a 2012 Buick on August 17, 2016.

(Year of vehicle is not correct. It should be <u>2002</u> and not 2016.)

Accurate:

A 16 year old boy was struck by a <u>2002</u> Buick on August 17, 2016.

Not complete:

A boy was struck by a 2002 Buick on August 17, 2016.

(Age of boy is missing.)

Complete:

A <u>16 year old boy</u> was struck by a 2002 Buick on August 17, 2016.

Question 7

Officer Ahren is asked to select the best summary (A, B, C, or D) of the following information: (The best summary is the one that expresses the information in the **most clear, accurate and complete manner**).

Place of accident: in front of 1726 West 8th Street, Tallahassee
Time of accident: 12:25 P.M.
Date of accident: September 11, 2016
Vehicle involved: 2006 Toyota
Driver: Cecilia Langer
Damage: cracked windshield
Details: A small branch fell from a tree and cracked the windshield of a 2006 Toyota.

-----

7. A. On September 11, 2016, in front of 1726 West 8th Street, Tallahassee, a small branch fell from a tree and cracked the windshield of a 2006 Toyota, owned by Cecilia Langer.

B. On September 11, 2016, in front of 1726 West 8th Street, Tallahassee, a small branch fell from a tree and cracked the windshield of a 2006 Toyota, driven by Cecilia Langer.

C. On September 11, 2016, at 12:52 P.M., in front of 1726 West 8ᵗʰ Street, Tallahassee, a small branch fell from a tree and cracked the windshield of a 2006 Toyota, driven by Cecilia Langer.

D. On September 11, 2016, at 12:25 P.M., in front of 1726 West 8ᵗʰ Street, Tallahassee, a small branch fell from a tree and cracked the windshield of a 2006 Toyota, driven by Cecilia Langer.

Written Expression Answer 7

Officer Ahren is asked to select the best summary (A, B, C, or D) of the following information: (The best summary is the one that expresses the information in the **most clear, accurate and complete manner).**

Place of accident: in front of 1726 West 8ᵗʰ Street, Tallahassee

Time of accident: 12:25 P.M.

Date of accident: September 11, 2016

Vehicle involved: 2006 Toyota

Driver: Cecilia Langer

Damage: cracked windshield

Details: A small branch fell from a tree and cracked the windshield of a 2006 Toyota.

-----

7. A. On September 11, 2016, in front of 1726 West 8ᵗʰ Street, Tallahassee, a small branch fell from a tree and cracked the windshield of a 2006 Toyota, <u>owned</u> by Cecilia Langer.

(WRONG because it states the car was "<u>owned</u>" by Cecilia Langer. The information says that Cecilia Langer was the "<u>driver</u>." Also, the time of the accident, 12:25 P.M., is not stated.)

B. On September 11, 2016, in front of 1726 West 8ᵗʰ Street, Tallahassee, a small branch fell from a tree and cracked the windshield of a 2006 Toyota, driven by Cecilia Langer.

(WRONG because the time of the accident, 12:25 P.M. is not stated.)

C. On September 11, 2016, at 12:52 P.M., in front of 1726 West 8ᵗʰ Street, Tallahassee, a small branch fell from a tree and cracked the windshield of a 2006 Toyota, driven by Cecilia Langer.

(WRONG because the time of the accident is wrong. The correct time is <u>12:25</u> P.M. and not <u>12:52</u> P.M.)

D. On September 11, 2016, at 12:25 P.M., in front of 1726 West 8th Street, Tallahassee, a small branch fell from a tree and cracked the windshield of a 2006 Toyota, driven by Cecilia Langer.
(CORRECT ANSWER. This is the only choice that contains all the information and does not contain any factual errors.)

Written Expression Question 8

Police Officer Slavik obtains the following information at the scene of a traffic accident:

Date of accident: July 4, 2016
Time of accident: 2:25 P.M.
Place of accident: intersection of 5th Avenue and 48th Street, Brooksville
Vehicles involved: 2007 Nissan and 2011 Buick
Drivers: Abe Molson (2007 Nissan) and Carol Soto (2011 Buick)
Damage: dent on driver's door of 2011 Buick

-----

8. Police Officer Slavik drafts four versions to express the above information. Which of the following four versions is most clear, accurate and complete?

A. On July 4, 2016, at 2:25 P.M., at the intersection of 5th Avenue and 48th Street, Brooksville, a 2007 Nissan and a 2011 Buick were involved in a traffic accident. The 2011 Buick, owned by Carol Soto, sustained a dent on the driver's door. The 2007 Nissan, driven by Abe Molson, did not sustain any damage.

B. At the intersection of 5th Avenue and 48th Street, Brooksville, a 2007 Nissan, owned by Abe Molson, and a 2011 Buick owned by Carol Soto, were involved in a car accident. The driver's door of the 2007 Nissan was dented. The accident occurred on July 4, 2016, at 2:25 P.M.

C. At the intersection of 5th Avenue and 48th Street, Brooksville, a 2007 Buick, owned by Abe Molson, and a 2011 Buick owned by Carol Soto, were involved in a car accident. The driver's door of the 2007 Nissan was dented. The accident occurred on July 4, 2016.

D. On July 4, 2016, at 2:25 P.M., at the intersection of 5th Avenue and 48th Street, Brooksville, a 2007 Nissan and a 2011 Buick were involved in a traffic accident. The 2011 Buick, driven by Carol Soto, sustained a dent on the driver's door. The 2007 Nissan, driven by Abe Molson, did not sustain any damage.

Written Expression Answer 8

Police Officer Slavik obtains the following information at the scene of a traffic accident:

Date of accident: July 4, 2016

Time of accident: 2:25 P.M.

Place of accident: intersection of 5th Avenue and 48th Street, Brooksville

Vehicles involved: 2007 Nissan and 2011 Buick

Drivers: Abe Molson (2007 Nissan) and Carol Soto (2011 Buick)

Damage: dent on driver's door of 2011 Buick

-----

8. Police Officer Slavik drafts four versions to express the above information. Which of the following four versions is most clear, accurate and complete?

A. On July 4, 2016, at 2:25 P.M., at the intersection of 5th Avenue and 48th Street, Brooksville, a 2007 Nissan and a 2011 Buick were involved in a traffic accident. The 2011 Buick, <u>owned by</u> Carol Soto, sustained a dent on the driver's door. The 2007 Nissan, driven by Abe Molson, did not sustain any damage.
(WRONG. This summary is not accurate. The 2011 Buick was <u>driven</u> by Carol Soto, not owned by her.)

B. At the intersection of 5th Avenue and 48th Street, Brooksville, a 2007 Nissan, owned by Abe Molson, and a 2011 Buick owned by Carol Soto, were involved in a car accident. <u>The driver's door of the 2007 Nissan was dented.</u> The accident occurred on July 4, 2016, at 2:25 P.M.
(WRONG. This summary is not accurate. The damage was to the 2011 Buick, not the 2007 Nissan. Also, the 2011 Buick was <u>driven</u> by Carol Soto, not <u>owned</u> by her, and the 2007 Nissan was <u>driven</u> by Abe Molson and not <u>owned</u> by him.)

C. At the intersection of 5th Avenue and 48th Street, Brooksville, a 2007 Buick, owned by Abe Molson, and a 2011 Buick owned by Carol Soto, were involved in a car accident. The driver's door of the 2007 Nissan was dented. The accident occurred on July 4, 2016.
(WRONG. This summary is incomplete and not accurate. The time of the accident, 2:25 P.M., is not stated. Also, the cars were <u>"driven by"</u> and not <u>"owned"</u> by the persons named.)

D. On July 4, 2016, at 2:25 P.M., at the intersection of 5th Avenue and 48th Street, Brooksville, a 2007 Nissan and a 2011 Buick were involved in a traffic accident. The 2011 Buick, driven by Carol Soto, sustained a dent on the driver's door. The 2007 Nissan, driven by Abe Molson, did not sustain any damage.
(CORRECT ANSWER. It contains all the information and has no errors.)

MEMORIZATION 5

These questions evaluate your ability to remember information that is provided in the form of pictures, numbers, procedures, etc.

You may be shown a picture and asked to examine it for a specified number of minutes (5 – 10 minutes). You will then be instructed not to look at the picture any longer and to answer 10-15 questions relating to details in the picture (Example: words, numbers, and images).

This question is probably not a type of question that you encountered during your school years. Because it may be different and new to you, it may be very helpful to practice answering such questions

Remember:

Memory is not dependent on intelligence or education.

Memorization is a skill and it can definitely be improved with practice!

MEMORIZATION

The methods of remembering details of a written passage or a picture are similar. In both cases, we can remember more if we concentrate on the details and organize the information into logical categories.

ORGANIZING INFORMATION INTO 5 CATEGORIES

1. WHO
Names or Titles of Persons

(Police Officers, pedestrians, children, drivers, perpetrators, ethnicity, race, etc.)

2. WHAT
(a scheduled event, accident, parade, protest, daily scene, store sales, etc.)

3. WHERE
(address, in front of, place, room, specific area....)

4. WHEN
(Date, event, special occasion; before/after)

5. WHY
(reason for scene, motivation of persons depicted, etc.)

REMEMBER:

Memory is <u>not</u> dependent on intelligence or education.

Memorization is a <u>skill</u> and it can definitely be improved with practice!

HOW CAN I PRACTICE MEMORY QUESTIONS?

Every day we are bombarded with a variety of pictures, including in newspapers, magazines and on the web.

Choose any picture from one of these sources and concentrate on it for ten minutes. Try to memorize as much detail as you can by using the organizing technique described above (or by any other method that helps you remember). Put the picture aside and do something else for another ten minutes. Then, without looking back at the picture, write down as much detail as you can remember – no matter how trivial. (Waiting for 10 minutes will help you reinforce your memory technique.)

Do at least one exercise each day. Choose different types of images. You will be surprised at how much your memory technique (and comfort level with this type of question) will improve.

The following pages contain four memory exercises. While doing the exercises, consider the following suggestions:

1. Study the picture carefully for the entire time that you are allowed to look at it.

2. Try to remember as much detail as you can. The more detail you can remember, the greater will be your chances of obtaining a higher score. Keep in mind that details that are relevant to the police officer job probably have a greater possibility of being the subject of memory questions.

3. Some memory experts suggest that you mentally divide the picture into 4 quarters and examine each quarter individually. They also suggest that after you finish examining each quarter, you quickly try to remember the details in the preceding quarters that you have memorized. During the memorization periods, try to repeat in your mind important details.

4. While you are trying to memorize the entire picture (or a quarter at a time) keep in mind the details of Who? What? Where? When? and Why?

5. As much as possible, arrange or group things and events in your mind.

6. If you find it helpful, close your eyes briefly and form a mental picture of the image.

7. If you feel that you have finished memorizing as much detail as possible and you still have more time to memorize, go back to the picture and memorize some more.

8. If appropriate and time permits, imagine yourself "walking through the scene." Many agree that after walking to a new place they have little trouble remembering the route.

———————

Memory is the mother of all wisdom.

- Aeschylus

Memory Exercise #1

Study the picture below for the next ten minutes. Try to remember as many details about the people and objects as you can. During the ten minutes, you are not permitted to take any notes or write anything.

At the end of ten minutes you will be asked to answer questions 1 – 10 (<u>without</u> looking back at the picture).

(After ten minutes)

Instructions for questions 1 – 10:

<u>Without</u> looking back at the picture, answer questions 1 – 10 on the following page.

(Note: These questions are intentionally difficult – probably harder than on the test.)

QUESTIONS

1. The number of people in the picture is:

A. 4   B. 5   C. 6   D. 7

2. How many of the males are wearing a hat?

A. 1   B. 2   C. 3   D. 4

3. Choose the best answer. The male wearing black sneakers is:

A. wearing white pants.   C. black.

B. not wearing sunglasses.   D. wearing a mostly white cap with a dark circle on it.

4. How many females are there in the picture?

A. 1   C. 3

B. 2   D. 4

5. With regard to the females:

A. Only one is wearing a necklace.   C. Both are wearing sunglasses.

B. Neither one is wearing a necklace.   D. none of the above

6. How many of the males are wearing sunglasses?

A. none   B. one   C. two   D. three

7. How many people are wearing sneakers?

A. 2   B. 3   C. 4   D. 5

8. How many of the females are wearing a white blouse?

A. none   B. one   C. two   D. three

9. How many males are wearing white T-shirts?

A. none   B. one   C. two   D. three

10. How many window-like openings are there in the walls behind the people?

A. one   C. three

B. two   D. four

_____

REMEMBERING THE PICTURE

How did you try to notice and remember the details in the picture?
As you looked at the picture, you may have been asking –

- What am I looking at?

   group of young people, in an alley, cement floor, brick building

- How many people are clearly visible?

   five (3 males and 2 females)

- What is common about some of the people?

   sunglasses

   3 men wearing hats

   1 man with a tight shirt

- Anything different or unusual?

   unusual pose, background seems to be an abandoned building

- What are the five people doing?

   posing for a photograph

- Anything else in the picture?

   two windows in the background, one open and without any shutter

   one woman with short T-shirt

   all are wearing sneakers

   all men have watches

ANSWERS

1. The number of people in the picture is:

A. 4　　　**B. 5**　　　C. 6　　　D. 7

2. How many of the males are wearing a hat?

A. 1　　　B. 2　　　**C. 3**　　　D. 4

3. Choose the best answer. The male wearing black sneakers is:

A. wearing white pants.　　　C. black.

B. not wearing sunglasses.　　　**D. wearing a mostly white cap with a dark circle on it.**

4. How many females are there in the picture?

A. 1　　　**B. 2**　　　C. 3　　　D. 4

5. With regard to the females:

A. Only one is wearing a necklace.　　　**C. Both are wearing sunglasses.**

B. Neither one is wearing a necklace.　　　D. none of the above

6. How many of the males are wearing sunglasses?

A. None　　　B. one　　　C. two　　　**D. three**

7. How many people are wearing sneakers?

A. 2　　　B. 3　　　C. 4　　　**D. 5**

8. How many of the females are wearing a white blouse?

A. none　　　B. one　　　C. two　　　D. three

9. How many males are wearing white T-shirts?

A. none　　　B. one　　　C. two　　　D. three

10. How many window-like openings are there in the walls behind the people?

A. one　　　C. three

B. two　　　D. four

Memory Exercise #2

Study the picture below for the next ten minutes. (Do not look at the questions). Try to remember as many details about the people and objects as you can. During the ten minutes, you are not permitted to take any notes or write anything.

At the end of ten minutes you will be asked to answer questions 1 – 10 (without looking back at the picture).

(After ten minutes)

Instructions for questions 1 – 10:

Without looking back at the picture, answer questions 1 – 10 on the following page.

(Note: These questions are intentionally difficult – probably harder than on the test.)

1. Choose the best answer: The mini-van (closest to you, the viewer) that is making a right turn is:

A. white with a checkered passenger door

B. all black

C. black with a checkered passenger door

D. all white

2. The man in the front who is carrying a white object is wearing:

A. a white jumpsuit

B. overalls

C. a black suit

D. none of the above

3 The woman closest to the front is:

A. carrying a black handbag.

B. carrying a white handbag.

C. carrying a black attaché case.

D. wearing long, black slacks

4. Above the head of the man with the dark suit who is carrying a white bag:

A. there is a street sign with the text "W 141 Street."

B. there is a street sign with the text "E 141 Street."

C. there is a street sign with the text "W 41 Street."

D. there is no street sign with visible text.

5. The vehicle between the two white vehicles in the front is:

A. a truck

B. a bus

C. a Ford convertible

D. none of the above

6. Choose the best answer: The approximate number of people on the left side of the picture is:

A. 3   B. 4   C. 5 or more, but less than 10   D. more than 20

7. What is correct about the three white minivans in the front of the picture?

A. All are making left turns.

B. All are making right turns.

C. They are all taxis.

D. none of the above

8. The number displayed on one of the buildings is:

A. 671

B. 761

B. 6717

D. none of the above

9. With regard to the sky:

A. It cannot be seen in the image.

B. It seems clear.

C. It is extremely cloudy.

D. none of the above.

10. On the sidewalk surface there is drawn:

A. An arrow pointing left (⟵).

B. An arrow pointing right (⟶).

C. A double arrow (⟷).

D. none of the above

"Genius is one percent inspiration and ninety-nine percent perspiration."

- Thomas Edison

ANSWERS

How did you try to notice and remember the details in the picture?

As you looked at the picture, you may have been asking –

- What am I looking at?

  city scene, large buildings, wide streets, vehicles, and pedestrians

- How many pedestrians are clearly visible?

  about 6 (4 males and 2 females)

- What is common about some pedestrians?

  dark clothes

  white shirts (men); some men with dark suits

  men with white shirts

- Anything different or unusual?

  a male is carrying a white bag, same color as a woman's pocketbook

- What are the cars doing?

  most are making turns

- What type of autos are they?

  3-4 mini-vans, several sedans

- Anything else in the picture?

  lamp posts, no street signs

  pavement is etched with rectangle designs

  some trees in the background

-----

1. Choose the best answer: The mini-van (closest to you, the viewer) that is making a right turn is:

A. white with a checkered passenger door

B. all black

C. black with a checkered passenger door

D. all white

2. The man in the front who is carrying a white object is wearing:

A. a white jumpsuit

B. overalls

C. a black suit

D. none of the above

3. The woman closest to the front is:

A. carrying a black handbag.

B. carrying a white handbag.

C. carrying a black attaché case.

D. wearing long, black slacks

4. Above the head of the man with the dark suit who is carrying a white bag:

A. there is a street sign with the text "W 141 Street."

B. there is a street sign with the text "E 141 Street."

C. there is a street sign with the text "W 41 Street."

D. there is no street sign with visible text.

5. The vehicle between the two white vehicles in the front is:

A. a truck

B. a bus

C. a Ford convertible

D. none of the above (a sedan)

6. Choose the best answer: The approximate number of people on the left side of the picture is:

A. 3   **C. 5 or more, but less than 10**

B. 4   D. more than 20

7. What is correct about the three white minivans in the front of the picture?

A. All are making left turns.

B. All are making right turns.

C. They are all taxis.

D. none of the above (Two are making right turns. One is making a left turn. None of them are taxis.)

8. The number displayed on one of the buildings is:

A. 671

B. 761

B. 6717

D. none of the above (No numbers are displayed.)

9. With regard to the sky:

A. It cannot be seen in the image.

B. It seems clear.

C. It is extremely cloudy.

D. none of the above.

10. On the sidewalk surface there is drawn:

A. An arrow pointing left (⟵).

B. An arrow pointing right (⟶).

C. A double arrow (⟷).

D. none of the above (No arrows are drawn on the sidewalk.)

_____

"I know the price of success: dedication, hard work and an unremitting devotion to the things you want to see happen."

-Frank Lloyd Wright

Memory Exercise #3

Study the picture below for the next ten minutes. Try to remember as many details about the people and objects as you can. During the ten minutes, you are not permitted to take any notes or write anything.

At the end of ten minutes you will be asked to answer questions 1 – 10 (**without** looking back at the picture).

(After ten minutes)

Instructions for questions 1 – 10:

Without looking back at the picture, answer questions 1 – 10 on the following page.

(Note: These questions are intentionally difficult – probably harder than on the test.)

1. The number of people very close to the drum of the cement truck is:
A. 4   B. 1   C. 2   D. 3

2. How many cranes are displayed in the picture?
A. 0   B. 1   C. 2   D. 3

3. The drum of the cement truck is:
A. white and with a dark stripe.   C. all black.
B. all white.   D. none of the above.

4. The building that is being worked on:
A. is fully scaffolded.   C. is 6 stories high.
B. is only partially scaffolded.   D. none of the above

5. Behind the building under construction, there is:
A. a parks scene.   C. a city skyline.
B. an airport.   D. none of the above.

6. The number of people on the ground is approximately:
A. 5 - 9   C. 13 - 15
B. 10 - 12   D. 16 - 20

7. In the sky there is clearly visible:
A. an airplane.   B. a helicopter.
C. a large bird.   D. none of the above.

8. How many cranes on the roof are lifting a horizontal object?
A. 0   C. 2
B. 1   D. 3

9. The excavator with a scoop full of dirt:
A. is near the middle of the picture.   B. is on the extreme left side of the picture.
C. has eight wheels.   D. being pulled by a tow truck.

10. Which of the following is in the picture?
A. a large advertising poster on the building's left side
B. a snack truck with a striped canopy
C. a camp trailer
D. none of the above

REMEMBERING THE PICTURE

How did you try to notice and remember the details in the picture?
As you looked at the picture, you may have been asking –

- What am I looking at?

　construction area of one building, tall buildings in the background, construction equipment, workers, cranes

- How many workers are clearly visible on the ground?

　seven or eight, one holding plans

- What is common about some workers?

　dark pants
　all of them seem busy working

- Anything different or unusual?

　All seem to be men (no women)

- What are the people doing?

　Unloading cement, pushing a wheel barrel, digging a hole, one looking at plans

- Anything else in the picture?

　two big sky cranes
　one white barreled cement mixer (with a red stripe)
　the building under construction has no windows yet
　both cranes are lifting a beam
　some workers are on the roof of the building
　there is scaffolding on the right side of the building

ANSWERS

1. The number of people very close to the drum of the cement truck is:
A. 4   C. 2
B. 1   D. 3

2. How many cranes are displayed in the picture?
A. 0   **C. 2**
B. 1   D. 3

3. The drum of the cement truck is:
A. white and with a dark stripe.   C. all black.
B. all white.   D. none of the above.

4. The building that is being worked on:
A. is fully scaffolded.   C. is 6 stories high.
B. is only partially scaffolded.   D. none of the above

5. Behind the building under construction, there is:
A. a parks scene.   **C. a city skyline.**
B. an airport.   D. none of the above.

6. The number of people on the ground is approximately:
A. 5 – 9   C. 13 - 15
B. 10 – 12   D. 16 - 20

7. In the sky there is clearly visible:
A. an airplane.   C. a large bird.
B. a helicopter   **D. none of the above.**

8. How many cranes on the roof are lifting a horizontal object?
A. 0   **C. 2**
B. 1   D. 3

9. The excavator with a scoop full of dirt:
A. is near the middle of the picture.   C. has eight wheels.
B. is on the extreme left side of the picture.   D. is being pulled by a tow truck.

10. Which of the following is in the picture?
A. a large advertising poster on the building's left side   C. a camp trailer
B. a snack truck with a striped canopy   **D. none of the above**

Memory Exercise #4

Study the picture below for the next ten minutes. Try to remember as many details about the people and objects as you can. During the ten minutes, you are not permitted to take any notes or write anything.

At the end of ten minutes you will be asked to answer questions 1 – 10 (<u>without</u> looking back at the picture).

(After ten minutes)

Instructions for questions 1 – 10:

<u>Without</u> looking back at the picture, answer questions 1 – 10 on the following page.

1. The number of buildings whose fronts are fully in the picture is:

A. 2   B. 3   C. 4   D. 5

2 The building with a sign that reads "ANTIQUES":

A. is in the center of the picture.   B. is the tallest building in the picture.

C. is a two-story building.   D. does not have an awning.

3. The building with the widest awning:

A. has two windows on the second floor.   B. has three windows on the second floor.

C. has four windows on the second floor.   D. has five windows on the second floor.

4. The American flag is attached to:

A. a window.   B. a lamppost

C. a garbage can   D. none of the above

5. How many outdoor garbage cans are there in the picture?

A. 1   B. 2   C. 3   D. 5

6. How many outdoor sitting benches are in the picture?

A. 1   B. 2   C. 3   D. 5

7. The sky can best be described as:

A. completely clear of clouds.   B. dark with lightning.

C. partly cloudy.   D. filled with rain.

8. The three buildings that are fully in the picture each have how many windows on the second floor?

A. 5   B. 2   C. 3   D. 1

9. How many buildings have fronts that are only partially in the picture?

A. 0   B. 1

C. 2   D. 3

10. How many lampposts are there in the picture?

A. 1   B. 2   C. 3   D. 5

Answers for Memory Exercise #4

1. The number of buildings whose fronts are fully in the picture is:

A. 2   **B. 3**   C. 4   D. 5

2 The building with a sign that reads "ANTIQUES":

A. is in the center of the picture.   B. is the tallest building in the picture.

C. is a two-story building.   D. does not have an awning.

3. The building with the widest awning:

A. has two windows on the second floor.   **B. has three windows on the second floor.**

C. has four windows on the second floor.   D. has five windows on the second floor.

4. The American flag is attached to:

A. a window.   **B. a lamppost**

C. a garbage can   D. none of the above

5. How many outdoor garbage cans are there in the picture?

A. 1   B. 2   C. 3   D. 5

6. How many outdoor sitting benches are in the picture?

A. 1   B. 2   C. 3   D. 5

7. The sky can best be described as:

A. completely clear of clouds.   B. dark with lightning.

C. partly cloudy.   D. filled with rain.

8. The three buildings that are fully in the picture each have how many windows on the second floor?

A. 5   B. 2   **C. 3**   D. 1

9. How many buildings have fronts that are only partially in the picture?

A. 0   B. 1

C. 2   D. 3

10. How many lampposts are there in the picture?

A. 1   B. 2   C. 3   D. 5

PROBLEM SENSITIVITY

6

These questions evaluate your ability to see the elements of a problem and also the problem in its entirety.

Problem sensitivity is important in a Police Officer's daily work. Spotting a possible problem developing during a patrol may aid the officer in preventing an incident or being ready if one does occur.

This type of question evaluates your ability to analyze different situations using personal experience, problem sensitivity and maturity of thought.

In one version of this type of question, rules or procedures may be presented along with a situation or incident in which the stated rules or procedures should be applied.

Another version of this type of question may present a number of "facts" (some conflicting), as stated by witnesses, victims or suspects. The candidate may be asked which description or account is not reliable, or which description or account is the most correct.

Questions 1 - 6

1. Police Officer Silvers is informed by a person who has just been mugged on the sidewalk that the perpetrator was a male with a pale complexion, about five feet ten inches tall and wearing a red T-shirt.

Officer Silvers looks down the street in an attempt to spot the perpetrator. According to the information provided by the victim, Police Officer Silvers should:

A. question all males and females on the street.

B. question all females wearing a red T-shirt.

C. question all persons of about the height of five feet ten inches.

D. question all light skinned males on the street who are wearing a red T-shirt and are about
   five feet ten inches tall.

----

2. Police Officer Horowitz notices that a heavy tree branch has fallen on lane 1 and lane 2 of a busy, four-lane highway. He has several traffic cones with him. Police Officer Horowitz should:

A. immediately barricade the four lanes to stop all traffic and thereby decrease the possibility of
   an accident.

B. immediately barricade three lanes with the cones and keep one lane open.

C. immediately barricade lanes three and four with the cones.

D. immediately barricade lanes one and two with the cones.

----

3. During his patrol, Police Officer David Swanson notices that a metal store sign approximately three feet wide and ten feet long has partially detached from the building and is dangerously close to crashing down to the crowded sidewalk, about twenty feet below.

Based on the preceding information, what is the first step that Police Officer Swanson should take?

A. Call for backup since he is on patrol alone.

B. Quickly get all persons away from the front of building.

C. Look at the sign for at least five minutes to determine when it will fall.

D. Go inside the store and notify the store owner.

FLORIDA LAW ENFORCEMENT BASIC ABILITIES TEST (BAT) EXAM GUIDE

4. Before you leave for patrol, your sergeant gives you written instructions which direct you to interview a Mr. Mary Boggs, owner of a bar and grill, regarding a complaint from the bar that youths from the neighborhood are breaking the bar windows when the bar is closed. You are confused about the identity (name and gender) of Mr. Mary Boggs. What is the first step you should take in this situation?

A. At the bar interview anyone named Boggs (male or female).

B. Disregard the sergeant's instructions as they are clearly confused.

C. Do not ask questions of the sergeant, as he might get upset.

D. Ask the sergeant for clarification of the name and gender of the owner of the bar.

----

5. Police Officer Susan Demitros is on patrol when she notices a man walking in an apparent daze in front of a liquor store. Because the man seems like he might collapse, Police Officer Demitros asks him if there is any problem. The man is clearly startled at being asked a question and hurriedly says, "I have no gun!" and quickly empties his pants pockets, which contained only a bottle of prescription pills which Officer Demitros knows are for anxiety. At that point the man loses consciousness and collapses, but Officer Demitros is able to catch him before he falls on the sidewalk.

Based on the preceding information, what should Police Officer Demitros do first?

A. Take the man into the liquor store and ask the owner if the man had just bought liquor.

B. Interview all nearby persons to determine if any are aware of this person ever having a gun.

C. Call for medical assistance.

D. Call the precinct to determine if the man has an arrest record, including DWI.

----

6. Prior to the start of your patrol, your sergeant gives you instructions which due to your distance from him, you do not hear part of the instructions. What should you do first?

A. Quickly carry out as many instructions as you can remember.

B. Ask your sergeant to repeat the instructions.

C. After you leave the precinct, ask a senior officer if he heard the instructions.

D. Carry out all instructions that you heard and then call the sergeant to ask him if you have completed all his instructions.

Answers 1 - 6

1. Police Officer Silvers is informed by a person who has just been mugged on the sidewalk that the perpetrator was a <u>male with a pale complexion</u>, about five feet ten inches tall and wearing a red T-shirt.

Officer Silvers looks down the street in an attempt to spot the perpetrator. According to the information provided by the victim, Police Officer Silvers should:

A. question all males and females on the street.

(WRONG. The description of a <u>male</u> with a pale complexion is specific. Questioning everyone is not called for and would likely result in wasted time and effort.)

B. question all females wearing a red T-shirt.

(WRONG. The description is of a <u>male</u>. Questioning females is not called for.)

C. question all persons of about the height of five feet ten inches.

(WRONG. The other details, "male" and "pale complexion," should be taken into consideration when deciding whom to question.)

D. question all light skinned males on the street who are wearing a red T-shirt and are about five feet ten inches tall.

(CORRECT. The description of these males matches the description of the alleged mugger.**)**

----

2. Police Officer Horowitz notices that a heavy tree branch has fallen on <u>lane 1 and lane 2</u> of a busy, four-lane highway. He has several traffic cones with him. Police Officer Horowitz should:

A. immediately barricade the four lanes to stop all traffic and thereby decrease the possibility of an accident.

(WRONG. The tree branch fell on lanes 1 and 2. Barricading the other two lanes is not necessary and could cause delays on the busy highway.)

B. immediately barricade three lanes with the cones and keep one lane open.

(WRONG. There is no apparent need to close the third lane.)

C. immediately barricade lanes three and four with the cones.

(WRONG. Lanes 1 and 2 (where the branch fell) should be barricaded, not the two lanes that are clear, lanes 3 and 4).

D. immediately barricade lanes one and two with the cones.

(CORRECT. These are the two lanes on which the branch has fallen and which need to be barricaded to reduce the possibility of accidents.)

----

3. During his patrol, Police Officer David Swanson notices that a metal store sign approximately three feet wide and ten feet long has partially detached from the building and is dangerously close to crashing down to the crowded sidewalk, about twenty feet below.

Based on the preceding information, what is the first step that Police Officer Swanson should take?

A. Call for backup since he is on patrol alone.

(WRONG. This is an emergency situation where the presence of additional officers will not address the immediate dangerous situation.)

B. Quickly get all persons away from the front of the building.

(CORRECT. The sign is "dangerously close to crashing to the crowded sidewalk, about twenty feet below." To prevent the possibility of injury, the officer should first concentrate on getting all persons away from the front of the building.)

C. Look at the sign for at least five minutes to determine when it will fall.

(WRONG. This is an emergency situation (people under the sign) that requires immediate action.)

D. Go inside the store and notify the store owner.

(WRONG. Officer Swanson should first warn the people who are in immediate danger.)

----

4. Before you leave for patrol, your sergeant gives you written instructions which direct you to interview a Mr. Mary Boggs, owner of a bar and grill, regarding a complaint from the bar that youths from the neighborhood are breaking the bar windows when the bar is closed. You are confused about the identity (name and gender) of Mr. Mary Boggs. What is the first step you should take in this situation?

A. At the bar interview anyone named Boggs (male or female).

(**WRONG.** You should get clarification from the sergeant of the correct name before going to the bar.)

B. Disregard the sergeant's instructions as they are clearly confused.

(**WRONG.** Orders from a superior should not be disregarded. You should ask for clarification.)

C. Do not ask questions of the sergeant, as he might get upset.

(**WRONG.** Questions should be asked if clarification is needed.)

D. Ask the sergeant for clarification of the name and gender of the owner of the bar.

(**CORRECT.** An officer should ask questions of a superior whenever clarification or additional relevant information is needed.)

----

5. Police Officer Susan Demitros is on patrol when she notices a man walking in an apparent daze in front of a liquor store. Because the man seems like he might collapse, Police Officer Demitros asks him if there is any problem. The man is clearly startled at being asked a question and hurriedly says, "I have no gun!" and quickly empties his pants pockets, which contained only a bottle of prescription pills which Officer Demitros knows are for anxiety. At that point <u>the man loses consciousness and collapses</u>, but Officer Demitros is able to catch him before he falls on the sidewalk.

Based on the preceding information, what should Police Officer Demitros do first?

A. Take the man into the liquor store and ask the owner if the man had just bought liquor.

(**WRONG.** Medical assistance is first required because the man lost consciousness.)

B. Interview all nearby persons to determine if any are aware of this person ever having a gun.

(**WRONG.** Medical assistance is first required. Any investigation should come after.)

C. Call for medical assistance.

(**CORRECT.** The man lost consciousness. This is a medical emergency. The correct action is to call for medical assistance.)

D. Call the precinct to determine if the man has an arrest record, including DWI.

(**WRONG.** Medical assistance is first required. Any investigation should come after.)

6. Prior to the start of your patrol, your sergeant gives you instructions which due to your distance from him, you do not hear part of the instructions. What should you do first?

A. Quickly carry out as many instructions as you can remember.

(WRONG. You should try to carry out all instructions from the sergeant, and not just those that you remember.)

B. Ask your sergeant to repeat the instructions.

(CORRECT. Asking for clarification is correct because this will help you understand all the instructions which you must follow.)

C. After you leave the precinct, ask a senior officer if he heard the instructions.

(WRONG. Any clarification should first come from the sergeant.)

D. Carry out all instructions that you heard and then call the sergeant to ask him if you have completed all his instructions.

(WRONG. You should get clarification as soon as possible, in this instance at the time that the sergeant gave the instructions.)

"There are no easy methods of learning difficult things; the method is to close your door, give out that you are not at home, and work."

– Joseph de Maistre

DEDUCTIVE REASONING

7

These questions evaluate your ability to understand general rules and apply them to specific situations.

Sometimes a question of this type may be difficult to answer, especially when the question involves a detailed procedure or complex section of law.

When answering a question of this type, try to understand fully the procedure or law. More than one reading may be necessary. As you read, try to see the relationships among the details provided.

Keep in mind that although it may be possible to answer very quickly some questions in other sections of the exam, the questions in this section may require more concentration and time.

Questions 1 - 3

Answer question 1 based on the information n provided in the following section of PL 120.60.

PL § 120.60 Stalking in the first degree

A person is guilty of stalking in the first degree when he or she commits the crime of stalking in the third degree as defined in subdivision three of section 120.50 or stalking in the second degree as defined in section 120.55 of this article and, in the course and furtherance thereof, he or she:

1. intentionally or recklessly causes physical injury to the victim of such crime, or

2. commits a class A misdemeanor defined in article one hundred thirty of this chapter, or a class E felony defined in section 130.25, 130.40 or 130.85 of this chapter, or a class D felony defined in section 130.30 or 130.45 of this chapter.

Stalking in the first degree is a class D felony.

-----

1. According to the preceding definition of stalking in the first degree, which of the following choices is an example of stalking in the first degree?

A. A male intentionally or recklessly causes physical injury to the victim of any crime.

B. A male or female commits a class A misdemeanor defined in article one hundred thirty of this chapter, or a class E felony defined in section 130.25, 130.40 or 130.85 of this chapter, or a class D felony defined in section 130.30 or 130.45 of this chapter (PL).

C. An adult intentionally or recklessly causes physical injury to the victim of a crime; or commits a class A misdemeanor defined in article one hundred thirty of this chapter, or a class E felony defined in section 130.25, 130.40 or 130.85 of this chapter, or a class D felony defined in section 130.30 or 130.45 of this chapter (PL).

D. none of the above

Answer question 2 based on the information provided in the following example of a Miranda Warning.

The following is an example of a Miranda Warning:

"You have the right to remain silent when questioned.

Anything you say or do may be used against you in a court of law.

You have the right to consult an attorney before speaking to the police and to have an attorney present during questioning now or in the future.

If you cannot afford an attorney, one will be appointed for you before any questioning, if you wish.

If you decide to answer any questions now, without an attorney present, you will still have the right to stop answering at any time until you talk to an attorney.

Knowing and understanding your rights as I have explained them to you, are you willing to answer my questions without an attorney present?"

-----

2. According to this version of the Miranda Warning, which of the following four choices is incorrect?

A. The person warned must be asked if he/she is willing to answer any questions without an attorney present after the person knows and understands his/her rights as explained.

B. The person must be informed that anything the person says or does may be used against the person in a court of law.

C. If the person cannot afford an attorney, one will be appointed only at the time of trial.

D. A person without an attorney present has the right to stop answering at any time until the person talks to an attorney.

Answer question 3 based on the information provided in the following section of CPL 720.10.

CPL § 720.10 Youthful offender procedure; definition of terms

As used in this article, the following terms have the following meanings:

1. "Youth" means a person charged with a crime alleged to have been committed when he was at least sixteen years old and less than nineteen years old or a person charged with being a juvenile offender (ages 13, 14 or 15) as defined in subdivision forty-two of section 1.20 of this chapter.

2. "Eligible youth" means a youth who is eligible to be found a youthful offender. Every youth is so eligible unless:

(a) the conviction to be replaced by a youthful offender finding is for (i) a class A-I or class A-II felony, or (ii) an armed felony as defined in subdivision forty-one of section 1.20, except as provided in subdivision three, or (iii) rape in the first degree, criminal sexual act in the first degree, or aggravated sexual abuse, except as provided in subdivision three, or

(b) such youth has previously been convicted and sentenced for a felony, or

(c) such youth has previously been adjudicated a youthful offender following conviction of a felony or has been adjudicated on or after September first, nineteen hundred seventy-eight a juvenile delinquent who committed a designated felony act as defined in the family court act.

-----

3. According to the preceding, which one of the following persons qualifies as an "eligible youth"?

A. Bernard Cranson, male, 20 years old, is arrested and charged with a crime. He was never found to be a juvenile offender.

B. Martin Frieds, male, 20 years old, is arrested and charged with a crime. He has previously been adjudicated a youthful offender following conviction of a felony.

C. Cecilia Norwin, a female, 17 years old, is arrested and charged with a crime. She had previously been adjudicated a youthful offender following a conviction and sentencing for a felony.

D. none of the above

Answers 1 - 3

Answer question 1 based on the information provided in the following section of PL 120.60.

PL § 120.60 Stalking in the first degree

A person is guilty of stalking in the first degree when he or she commits the crime of stalking in the third degree as defined in subdivision three of section 120.50 or stalking in the second degree as defined in section 120.55 of this article <u>and, in the course and furtherance thereof, he or she:</u>

1. intentionally or recklessly causes physical injury to the victim of such crime, or

2. commits a class A misdemeanor defined in article one hundred thirty of this chapter, or a class E felony defined in section 130.25, 130.40 or 130.85 of this chapter, or a class D felony defined in section 130.30 or 130.45 of this chapter.

Stalking in the first degree is a class D felony.

A couple of careful readings of the preceding section of law can help us to summarize it as follows:

A person is guilty of stalking in the first degree **IF** the person in the process of committing the crime of stalking in the second degree or stalking in the third degree **ALSO** does at least one of the following:

1. intentionally or recklessly causes physical injury to the victim of the second or third degree stalking, OR

2. commits one of the specific A misdemeanors or E felonies listed in PL 120.60.

Stalking in the first degree is a class D felony.

1. According to the preceding definition of stalking in the first degree, which of the following choices is an example of stalking in the first degree?

A. A male intentionally or recklessly causes physical injury to the victim of any crime.

(WRONG. According to our summary, the physical injury must be in the course of committing stalking in the second degree or stalking in the third degree and other specified offense.)

B. A male or female commits a class A misdemeanor defined in article one hundred thirty of this chapter, or a class E felony defined in section 130.25, 130.40 or 130.85 of this chapter, or a class D felony defined in section 130.30 or 130.45 of this chapter (PL).

(WRONG. According to our summary, the offense must be in the course of committing stalking in the second degree or stalking in the third degree.)

C. An adult intentionally or recklessly causes physical injury to the victim of a crime; or commits a class A misdemeanor defined in article one hundred thirty of this chapter, or a class E felony defined in section 130.25, 130.40 or 130.85 of this chapter, or a class D felony defined in section 130.30 or 130.45 of this chapter (PL).

(WRONG. According to our summary, the physical injury must be in the course of committing stalking in the second degree or stalking in the third degree.)

D. none of the above

(THIS IS THE RIGHT CHOICE. All the other choices ("A", "B," and "C") do not consider that the physical injury or commission of any of the specified crimes must be during the commission of stalking in the second degree or stalking in the third degree.)

Answer question 2 based on the information provided in the following example of a Miranda Warning.

The following is an example of a Miranda Warning:

"You have the right to remain silent when questioned.

Anything you say or do may be used against you in a court of law.

You have the right to consult an attorney before speaking to the police and to have an attorney present during questioning now or in the future.

If you cannot afford an attorney, one will be appointed for you before any questioning, if you wish.

If you decide to answer any questions now, without an attorney present, you will still have the right to stop answering at any time until you talk to an attorney.

Knowing and understanding your rights as I have explained them to you, are you willing to answer my questions without an attorney present?"

-----

2. According to this version of the Miranda Warning, which of the following four choices is incorrect?

A. The person warned must be asked if he/she is willing to answer any questions without an attorney present after the person knows and understands his/her rights as explained.

(CORRECT STATEMENT. The last sentence states, "Knowing and understanding your rights as I have explained them to you, are you willing to answer my questions without an attorney present?" Statement "A" is therefore a correct statement and not the incorrect statement that we are looking for.)

B. The person must be informed that anything the person says or does may be used against the person in a court of law.

(CORRECT STATEMENT. Sentence two states, "Anything you say or do may be used against you in a court of law." Statement "B" is therefore a correct statement and not the incorrect statement that we are looking for.)

C. If the person cannot afford an attorney, one will be appointed only at the time of trial.

(INCORRECT STATEMENT. Therefore, "C" is the answer. Sentence four states, "If you cannot afford an attorney, one will be appointed for you <u>before any questioning</u>, if you wish.")

D. A person without an attorney present has the right to stop answering at any time until the person talks to an attorney.

(CORRECT STATEMENT. Sentence five states, "If you decide to answer any questions now, without an attorney present, you will still have the right to stop answering at any time until you talk to an attorney." Statement "D" is therefore a correct statement and not the incorrect statement that we are looking for.)

Answer question 3 based on the information provided in the following section of CPL 720.10.

CPL § 720.10 Youthful offender procedure; definition of terms

As used in this article, the following terms have the following meanings:

1. "Youth" means a person charged with a crime alleged to have been committed when he was at least sixteen years old and less than nineteen years old or a person charged with being a juvenile offender (ages 13, 14 or 15) as defined in subdivision forty-two of section 1.20 of this chapter.

2. "Eligible youth" means a youth who is eligible to be found a youthful offender. Every youth is so eligible unless:

(a) the conviction to be replaced by a youthful offender finding is for (i) a class A-I or class A-II felony, or (ii) an armed felony as defined in subdivision forty-one of section 1.20, except as provided in subdivision three, or (iii) rape in the first degree, criminal sexual act in the first degree, or aggravated sexual abuse, except as provided in subdivision three, or

(b) such youth has previously been convicted and sentenced for a felony, or

(c) such youth has previously been adjudicated a youthful offender following conviction of a felony or has been adjudicated on or after September first, nineteen hundred seventy-eight a juvenile delinquent who committed a designated felony act as defined in the family court act.

3, According to the preceding, which one of the following persons qualifies as an "eligible youth"?

A. Bernard Cranson, male, 20 years old, is arrested and charged with a crime. He was never found to be a juvenile offender.

(DOES NOT QUALIFY. The youth has to be less than 19 years old (See "1" in section 720.10)

B. Martin Frieds, male, 20 years old, is arrested and charged with a crime. He has previously been adjudicated a youthful offender following conviction of a felony.

(DOES NOT QUALIFY. The youth has to be less than 19 years old (See "1" in section 720.10).

C. Cecilia Norwin, a female, 17 years old, is arrested and charged with a crime. She had previously been convicted and sentenced for a felony.

(DOES NOT QUALIFY. The section states, "2. Eligible youth means a youth who is eligible to be found a youthful offender. Every youth is so eligible **unless**... (b) such youth has previously been adjudicated a youthful offender following a conviction and sentencing for a felony." Ms. Norwin was previously convicted and sentenced for a felony.)

D. none of the above

(THIS IS THE ANSWER because none of the preceding three persons qualify as a youthful offender.)

> "In a major matter, no details are small."
> - Paul De Gondi

The question on the next page tests your ability to pay attention to detail.

Question 4

Below is a drawing of a "Revolver" and 4 more drawings of revolvers (A, B, C, and D). Which of the four drawings (A, B, C, D) best matches the drawing of the "Revolver"?

Revolver

A.

B.

C.

D.

4. The drawing which best matches the drawing of the "Revolver" is:

    A. Drawing A   B. Drawing B

    C. Drawing C   D. Drawing D

Answer 4

Below is a drawing of a "Revolver" and 4 more drawings of revolvers (A, B, C, and D). Which of the four drawings (A, B, C, D) best matches the drawing of the "Revolver"?

4. The drawing which best matches the drawing of the "Revolver" is:

A. Drawing A   B. Drawing B

C. Drawing C   **D. Drawing D**

Questions 5 - 6

Answer questions 5 - 6 based on the information provided in the following summaries of two Penal Law and Criminal Procedure Law sections.

Penal Law (PL) S 240.40 Appearance in public under the influence of narcotics or a drug other than alcohol.

A person is guilty of appearance in public under the influence of narcotics or a drug other than alcohol when he appears in a public place under the influence of narcotics or a drug other than alcohol to the degree that he may endanger himself or other persons or property, or annoy persons in his vicinity. Appearance in public under the influence of narcotics or a drug other than alcohol is a violation.

Criminal Procedure Law (CPL) S 160.10 When fingerprints may or must be taken

Following an arrest, or following arraignment upon a local criminal court accusatory instrument, a defendant must be fingerprinted where the accusatory instrument charges:

(a) a felony

(b) a misdemeanor defined in the Penal Law

(c) a misdemeanor defined outside of the Penal Law which would constitute a felony if such person had a previous judgment of conviction for a crime

(d) loitering for the purposes of engaging in a prostitution offense (Penal Law 240.37)

After an arrest for any offense, fingerprints may be taken where:

(a) law enforcement is unable to ascertain the person's identity.

(b) identification given by such person may not be accurate.

(c) there is reasonable cause to believe the person might be sought by law enforcement officials for the commission of some other offense.

When fingerprints are required to be taken, photographs and palm prints may be taken.

-----

5. Police Officer Marino arrests a person whom he reasonably believes is appearing in public under the influence of narcotics or a drug other than alcohol and who is annoying persons in his vicinity. The person provides acceptable I.D. (FL. issued driver's license with photo).

Which of the following choices is correct with respect to requiring fingerprints from the person arrested?

A. Fingerprints must be taken because the person was arrested for an offense.

B. Because fingerprints are required for any arrest as per PL S 240.0, photographs and palm prints may be taken.

C. Fingerprints must be taken because all drug offenses are felonies.

D. CPL S 160.10 does not authorize the taking of fingerprints in this instance.

----

6. Police Officer Janet Yaeger arrests a person for loitering for the purposes of engaging in a prostitution offense (Penal Law 240.37). Which of the following four statements is correct?

A. Fingerprints must be taken only if the person is of the age of 18 or over.

B. Fingerprints can only be taken if photographs and palm prints are also taken.

C. Fingerprints must be taken, even if Officer Yaeger personally knows the identity of the person arrested.

D. Photographs and palm prints must be taken.

Answers 5 - 6

5. Police Officer Marino arrests a person whom he reasonably believes is appearing in public under the influence of narcotics or a drug other than alcohol and who is annoying persons in his vicinity. The person provides acceptable I.D. (FL. issued driver's license with photo).

Which of the following choices is correct with respect to requiring fingerprints from the person arrested?

A. Fingerprints must be taken because the person was arrested for an offense.

(WRONG. Fingerprints must be taken when the arrest is for specified offenses ((a)-(d)) and not for just any offense.)

B. Because fingerprints are required for an arrest as per PL S 240.40, photographs and palm prints may be taken.

(WRONG. PL 240.40 is for a violation (and is not an offense listed in CPL 160.10 ((a)-(d))

C. Fingerprints must be taken because all drug offenses are felonies.

(WRONG. All drug offenses are not felonies. One example is PL S 240, a violation.)

D. CPL S 160.10 does not authorize the taking of fingerprints in this instance.

(CORRECT. The offense is a violation, and not an offense specified in CPL 160.10 ((a)-(d)).

6. Police Officer Janet Yaeger arrests a person for loitering for the purposes of engaging in a prostitution offense (Penal Law 240.37). Which of the following four statements is correct?

A. Fingerprints must be taken only if the person is of the age of 18 or over.

(WRONG. CPL 160.10 does not specify any minimum age.)

B. Fingerprints can only be taken if photographs and palm prints are also taken.

(WRONG. CPL 160.10 states, "When fingerprints are required to be taken, photographs and palm prints <u>may</u> be taken" – the reverse meaning of answer B.)

C. Fingerprints must be taken, even if Officer Yaeger personally knows the identity of the person arrested.

(CORRECT. CPL 160.10 states "Following an arrest, or following arraignment upon a local criminal court accusatory instrument, a defendant <u>must</u> be fingerprinted where the accusatory instrument charges...<u>loitering for purposes of engaging in a prostitution offense</u>....")

D. Photographs and palm prints must be taken.

(WRONG. CPL 160.10 states, "When fingerprints are required to be taken, photographs and palm prints <u>may</u> be taken.")

"I know the price of success: dedication, hard work and an unremitting devotion to the things you want to see happen."

- Frank Lloyd Wright

Answer Questions 7 - 8 based on the following map.

In answering the questions, follow the flow of traffic, as indicated by the arrows. Names of streets, buildings, public areas, and points 1-9 are indicated on the map.

7. Imagine that you are at Elm Street and Ingersoll Avenue and then drive west to Hargrove Avenue, then turn north to Dorance St., then travel east to Ingersoll Avenue, then travel north to Lincoln St. You will be closest to which one of the following points?

A. 2   B. 4   C. 5   D. 7

8. If you start your drive at point number 6, then drive west to Ingersoll Avenue, then drive north to Dorance St., then east to Franklin Avenue, then drive north to Fairfield St., you will be closest to which one of the following points?

A. 4   B. 5   C. 7   D. 2

7. Imagine that you are at Elm Street and Ingersoll Avenue and then drive west to Hargrove Avenue, then turn north to Dorance St., then travel east to Ingersoll Avenue, then travel north to Lincoln St. You will be closest to which one of the following points?

A. 2   **B. 4**   C. 5   D. 7

(The route is indicated by dark arrows.)

Answer for Question 8

8. If you start your drive at point number 6, then drive west to Ingersoll Avenue, then drive north to Dorance St., then east to Franklin Avenue, then drive north to Fairfield St., you will be closest to which one of the following points?

A. 4   B. 5   **C. 7**   D. 2

(The route is indicated by dark arrows.)

Questions 9 - 14

Answer questions 9 and 10 based on the preceding map.

9. You are driving south in your patrol car and you are at the intersection of Lincoln St. and Ingersoll Avenue. You are informed that an auto accident has just occurred at the intersection of Lincoln St. and Hargrove Avenue. Assuming that you must obey all traffic signs, which one of the following four choices describes the most direct route?

A. Drive straight west to the intersection of Lincoln St. and Hargrove Avenue, one block away.

B. Drive east to Franklin Avenue, then south on Franklin Avenue to Fairfield Street, then west on Fairfield St. to Hargrove Avenue, then north on Hargrove Avenue to the intersection of Lincoln St. and Hargrove Avenue.

C. Drive straight east to the intersection of Lincoln St. and Hargrove Avenue, one block away.

D. Drive south on Ingersoll Avenue to Fairfield St, then drive west on Fairfield St. to Hargrove Avenue, then north to the intersection of Lincoln St. and Hargrove Avenue.

----

10. You are driving north in your patrol car and you are at Hargrove Avenue and E St. You are informed that a building is on the verge of collapsing at the corner of Lincoln St. and Franklin Avenue. Which one of the following four choices describes the most direct route?

A. Drive east on Lincoln St. to the corner of Lincoln St. and Franklin Avenue.

B. Drive south to Lincoln St., then right on Lincoln St. to the corner of Lincoln St. and Franklin Avenue.

C. Drive south to Lincoln St., then right on Lincoln St. to the corner of Lincoln St. and Franklin Avenue.

D. Drive north to Lincoln St., then right on Lincoln St. and continue to the corner of Lincoln St. and Franklin Avenue.

Answer question 11 based on the following information:

During the month of July 2016 there were 9 burglaries reported in Police Officer Callion's precinct. In two of the burglaries, neighbors reported that at the approximate time of the burglaries they witnessed a male white, average height, shoulder length, dark hair, "with about a one inch scar on his left cheek." Both times the man was carrying a large brown carton out of the residence that had been burglarized. They also reported that at both times he had been wearing a blue T-shirt, dark blue, dirty dungarees, and white sneakers.

-----

11. During his patrol, Officer Callion stops four white males for questioning. He had recorded in his memo book the description given by the two witnesses. Which piece of information should Officer Callion consider the most important and pay careful attention to in identifying the suspected burglar?

A. the dark blue, dirty dungarees

B. the shoulder length, dark hair

C. the approximately one inch scar on his left cheek

D. the blue T-shirt

Answer question 12 based on the following information:

Prior to the start of his patrol, Officer Kevin Johnson learns at the precinct that a female, about 65 years old, had been mugged one hour earlier by a person who the victim described as a "white young man, about twenty years old, with dark hair tied in a shoulder length ponytail, and with severe acne on his face." She also described him as wearing black pants, a yellow T-shirt, and black sneakers.

-----

12. During his patrol, Officer Johnson sees a group of six white males, about 20-25 years old, standing in front of Ernie's Bar. Officer Johnson stops his patrol car about twenty feet away to get a better look at the six males. Which of the following parts of the description provided by the victim is most important for Officer Johnson to consider in his attempt to identify the possible suspect?

A. the yellow T-shirt

B. the shoulder length pony tail

C. the black sneakers

D. the acne on the alleged mugger

Answer questions 13 - 14 based on the following information:

Police Officer Gravitz is assigned to patrol an area which includes four Housing Developments. During the prior four weeks, crime statistics show that four burglaries were reported at the Bellman Housing Development, all between the hours of 10:00 a.m. and 4:00 p.m. At the Diamond Housing Development ten robberies were reported. At the Adrian Housing Development seven mailboxes were broken into. At the Garnacy Housing Development four bicycles were stolen. The robberies all occurred between 9:30 a.m. and 4:30 p.m. The mailboxes were broken into between 9:30 a.m. and 10:30 a.m. The bicycles were all reported stolen in the afternoon and before 5:00 p.m.

13. Officer Gravitz works the 9:00 a.m. to 5:00 p.m. tour. On Monday, his sergeant instructs him to pay careful attention to robberies. To try to reduce the number of robberies, Office Gravitz should patrol the:

A. Garnacy Housing Development

B. Bellman Housing Development

C. Adrian Housing Development

D. Diamond Housing Development

----

14. On Tuesday Officer Gravitz also works the 9:00 a.m. to 5:00 p.m. tour. On Tuesday, his sergeant tells him that three more mailboxes have been broken into at the same housing development that reported the prior break-ins and instructs him to pay careful attention to mailbox break-ins. To try to reduce the number of break-ins of mailboxes, Office Gravitz should patrol the:

A. Garnacy Housing Development

B. Bellman Housing Development

C. Adrian Housing Development

D. Diamond Housing Development

"An investment in knowledge always pays the best interest."

- Benjamin Franklin

Answer for Question 9

9. You are driving south in your patrol car and you are at the intersection of Lincoln St. and Ingersoll Avenue. You are informed that an auto accident has just occurred at the intersection of Lincoln St. and Hargrove Avenue. Assuming that you must obey all traffic signs, which one of the following four choices describes the most direct route?

A. Drive straight west to the intersection of Lincoln St. and Hargrove Avenue, one block away.

B. Drive east to Franklin Avenue, then south on Franklin Avenue to Fairfield Street, then west on Fairfield St. to Hargrove Avenue, then north on Hargrove Avenue to the intersection of Lincoln St. and Hargrove Avenue.

C. Drive straight east to the intersection of Lincoln St. and Hargrove Avenue, one block away.

D. Drive south on Ingersoll Avenue to Fairfield St, then drive west on Fairfield St. to Hargrove Avenue, then north to the intersection of Lincoln St. and Hargrove Avenue.

Answer for Question 10

10. You are driving north in your patrol car and you are at Hargrove Avenue and E St. You are informed that a building is on the verge of collapsing at the corner of Lincoln St. and Franklin Avenue. Which one of the following four choices describes the most direct route?

A. Drive east on Lincoln St. to the corner of Lincoln St. and Franklin Avenue.

B. Drive south to Lincoln St., then right on Lincoln St. to the corner of Lincoln St. and Franklin Avenue.

C. Drive south to Lincoln St., then right on Lincoln St. to the corner of Lincoln St. and Franklin Avenue.

D. Drive north to Lincoln St., then right on Lincoln St. and continue to the corner of Lincoln St. and Franklin Avenue.

Answers 11 - 14

Answer question 11 based on the following information:

During the month of July 2016 there were 9 burglaries reported in Police Officer Callion's precinct. In two of the burglaries, neighbors reported that at the approximate time of the burglaries they witnessed a male white, average height, shoulder length, dark hair, "with about a one inch scar on his left cheek." Both times the man was carrying a large brown carton out of the residence that had been burglarized. They also reported that at both times he had been wearing a blue T-shirt, dark blue, dirty dungarees, and white sneakers.

-----

11. During his patrol, Officer Callion stops four white males for questioning. He had recorded in his memo book the description given by the two witnesses. Which piece of information should Officer Callion consider the most important and pay careful attention to in identifying the suspected burglar?

A. the dark blue, dirty dungarees

(WRONG. A suspect can easily change dungarees. Also, many men wear blue, and sometimes dirty, dungarees.)

B. the shoulder length, dark hair

(WRONG. Although the length of the hair may be useful, a suspect can easily change the length of the hair or the hair style.)

C. the approximately one inch scar on his left cheek

(CORRECT. This is the best answer because a scar cannot easily be changed or hidden.)

D. the blue T-shirt

(WRONG. A suspect can easily change his T-shirt. Also, blue T-shirts are common.)

Answer question 12 based on the following information:

Prior to the start of his patrol, Officer Kevin Johnson learns at the precinct that a female, about 65 years old, had been mugged one hour earlier by a person who the victim described as a "white young man, about twenty years old, with dark hair tied in a shoulder length ponytail, and with severe acne on his face." She also described him as wearing black pants, a yellow T-shirt, and black sneakers.

12. During his patrol, Officer Johnson sees a group of six white males, about 20-25 years old, standing in front of Ernie's Bar. Officer Johnson stops his patrol car about twenty feet away to get a better look at the six males. Which of the following parts of the description provided by the victim is most important for Officer Johnson to consider in his attempt to identify the possible suspect?

A. the yellow T-shirt

(WRONG. A suspect can easily change his T-shirt.)

B. the shoulder length pony tail

(WRONG. Although the length of the hair may be useful, a suspect can easily change the length of the hair or the hair style.)

C. the black sneakers

(WRONG. A suspect can easily change his sneakers. Also, many men wear black sneakers.)

D. the acne on the alleged mugger

(CORRECT. This is the best answer because acne cannot easily be changed or hidden.)

Answer questions 13 - 14 based on the following information:

Police Officer Gravitz is assigned to patrol an area which includes four Housing Developments. During the prior four weeks, crime statistics show that four burglaries were reported at the Bellman Housing Development, all between the hours of 10:00 a.m. and 4:00 p.m. At the Diamond Housing Development ten robberies were reported. At the Adrian Housing Development seven mailboxes were broken into. At the Garnacy Housing Development four bicycles were stolen. The robberies all occurred between 9:30 a.m. and 4:30 p.m. The mailboxes were broken into between 9:30 a.m. and 10:30 a.m. The bicycles were all reported stolen in the afternoon and before 5:00 p.m.

-----

13. Officer Gravitz works the 9:00 a.m. to 5:00 p.m. tour. On Monday, his sergeant instructs him to pay careful attention to robberies. To try to reduce the number of robberies, Office Gravitz should patrol the:

A. Garnacy Housing Development

(WRONG. At the Garnacy Housing Development four bicycles were stolen.)

B. Bellman Housing Development

(WRONG ... four <u>burglaries</u> were reported at the Bellman Housing Development....)

C. Adrian Housing Development

(WRONG. At the Adrian Housing Development seven <u>mailboxes</u> were broken into.)

D. Diamond Housing Development

(CORRECT. "At the Diamond Housing Development ten <u>robberies</u> were reported." He should patrol this development because it is the most likely housing development to have robberies.)

----

14. On Tuesday Officer Gravitz also works the 9:00 a.m. to 5:00 p.m. tour. On Tuesday, his sergeant tells him that three more mailboxes have been broken into at the same housing development that reported the prior break-ins and instructs him to pay careful attention to mailbox break-ins. To try to reduce the number of break-ins of mailboxes, Office Gravitz should patrol the:

A. Garnacy Housing Development

(WRONG. "At the Garnacy Housing Development four <u>bicycles</u> were stolen.")

B. Bellman Housing Development

(WRONG. "... four <u>burglaries</u> were reported at the Bellman Housing Development....")

C. Adrian Housing Development

(CORRECT. During the prior four weeks, "At the Adrian Housing Development seven <u>mailboxes</u> were broken into.")

D. Diamond Housing Development

(WRONG. "At the Diamond Housing Development ten <u>robberies</u> were reported.")

"Success is the sum of all small efforts, repeated day in and day out."

- Robert Collier

INDUCTIVE REASONING

8

These questions test your ability to combine details or separate pieces of information to form general rules or a conclusion so that you may correctly answer a question based on a scenario that is provided.

The information provided may include sections of law, procedures, policies, or situations.

More than one careful reading of the information may be necessary before answering the question.

Question 1

Time Limitations for the Commencement of a Criminal Action

Type of Offense	For the commencement of a criminal action to be timely, an accusatory instrument must be filed within the following time periods after the commission of the offense
Class "A" felony (or rape in the first degree (130.35 PL), or criminal sexual act in the first degree (130.50 PL), or aggravated sexual abuse in the first degree (130.70 PL) or sexual conduct against a child in the first degree	any time
any other felony	within 5 years
misdemeanor	within 2 years
petty offense	within 1 year

1. Based on the above table, which of the following statements is not correct?

A. Prosecution for any felony must be commenced within 5 years of commission of the offense.

B. Where the offense is a misdemeanor, for the commencement of a criminal action to be timely, an accusatory instrument must be filed within 2 years following the commission of the offense.

C. Where the offense charged is aggravated sexual abuse in first degree (130.70 PL), for the commencement of a criminal action to be timely, an accusatory instrument may be filed at any time following the commission of the offense.

D. Where the offense is a petty offense, for the commencement of a criminal action to be timely, an accusatory instrument must be filed within 1 year following the commission of the offense.

Answer 1

A. Prosecution for any felony must be commenced within 5 years of commission of the offense.

The statement is <u>not</u> correct because for certain felonies the prosecution can begin at <u>any</u> time after the offense is committed. These felonies are: "Class "A" felony (or rape in the first degree (130.35 PL), or criminal sexual act in the first degree (130.50 PL), or aggravated sexual abuse in the first degree (130.70 PL) or sexual conduct against a child in the first degree)."

Inductive Reasoning Questions 2 - 3

Answer questions 2 - 3 based on the following summary of "CPL 100.10 Definitions of Local Criminal Court Accusatory Instruments."

CPL 100.10 Definitions of Local Criminal Court accusatory instruments

    1. An **Information** is a verified written accusation by a person, charging person(s) with offense(s), none of which is a felony. It may serve as the basis for the commencement of an action and for prosecution.

    2. A **Simplified information** is a written accusation by a police officer (or other public servant authorized to issue a simplified information).

        1. A **Simplified parks information** charges parks/recreation offense(s) less than a felony.

        2. A **Simplified environmental conservation information** charges environmental conservation offense(s) less than a felony.

        3. A **Simplified traffic information** charges traffic infractions or misdemeanors.

    3. A **Prosecutor's information** is a written accusation filed by the DA, either at the direction of the grand jury or at the direction of the local criminal court, or at the DA's own instance, and charges offense(s) less than a felony.

    4. A **Misdemeanor complaint** is a verified written accusation by a person charging offense(s), at least one of which is a misdemeanor, and none is a felony.

5. A **Felony complaint** is a verified written accusation by a person which charges offense(s), one or more of which must be felonies.

-----

2. Based on the preceding (CPL 100.10) definitions, which of the following statements is correct?

A. A Prosecutor's information is the same as a misdemeanor complaint.

B. A felony complaint must be filed by the D.A.

C. A Simplified Parks Information charges a felony.

D. A felony complaint charges at least one felony.

----

3. Police Officer Gonzalez is reviewing the above definitions sheet of Local Criminal Court accusatory instruments. Based on the definitions, he may correctly conclude that:

A. All accusatory instruments can charge any offense.

B. Simplified informations may be issued by all citizens.

C. Prosecutor's informations and misdemeanor complaints can charge misdemeanors and felonies.

D. None of the above.

Answers 2 - 3

2. Based on the preceding (CPL 100.10) definitions, which of the following statements is correct?

A. A Prosecutor's information is the same as a misdemeanor complaint.

(WRONG. A Prosecutor's Information is a written accusation by the D.A., whereas a misdemeanor complaint is a written accusation by a person.)

B. A felony complaint must be filed by the D.A.

(WRONG. A felony complaint is a written accusation by a person.)

C. A Simplified Parks Information charges a felony.

(WRONG. A Simplified Parks Information charges less than a felony.)

D. A felony complaint charges at least one felony.

(CORRECT. A felony complaint is a verified written accusation by a person which charges offense(s), <u>one or more of which must be felonies</u>.)

----

3. Police Officer Gonzalez is reviewing the above definitions sheet of Local Criminal Court accusatory instruments. Based on the definitions, he may correctly conclude that:

A. All accusatory instruments can charge any offense.

(WRONG. Accusatory instruments can charge only <u>specified</u> offenses.)

B. Simplified informations may be issued by all citizens.

(WRONG. Simplified informations can be issued only by a <u>police officer</u> or by other <u>authorized public servants</u>.)

C. Prosecutor's informations and misdemeanor complaints can charge misdemeanors and felonies.

(WRONG. Prosecutor's informations and misdemeanor complaints <u>cannot charge felonies</u>.)

D. None of the above.

(CORRECT ANSWER. All other choices are incorrect.)

Questions 4 - 5

4. While you are on patrol, a male, about 21 years old, reports that he had chained his bicycle to a bicycle parking station and gone into a drugstore to purchase shampoo, only to discover when he came out of the store that his bicycle chain had been cut and his bicycle stolen. You question four witnesses who give you four statements. Which of the following four statements is most likely to be incorrect?

A. The person who cut the chain and rode away with the bicycle was a male, white, about 21 years old and about six feet tall. He was wearing white sneakers, blue dungarees, a yellow T-shirt, and a dark brown backpack. He headed north for one block and then made a left turn.

B. The person who cut the chain was a male, white, about six feet tall. He was wearing black sneakers, blue dungarees, a yellow T-shirt, and a dark brown backpack. He rode the bicycle north for one block and then made a left turn.

C. The person who cut the chain and rode away with the bicycle was a male, white, about six feet tall. He was wearing black sneakers, blue dungarees, a yellow T-shirt, and a dark brown backpack. He pedaled north for one block and then made a left turn.

D. The person who cut the chain and rode away with the bicycle was a male, white, about six feet tall. He was wearing black sneakers, blue dungarees, a yellow T-shirt, and a dark brown backpack. He headed north for one block and then made a left turn.

----

5. Four witnesses to a hit and run accident tell Police Officer Tumi that they memorized the license plate of the car that sped away from the accident. Which of the following is the most like to be correct?

A. 9237SFG

B. 9587SFG

C. 9537SFG

D. 9531SFG

Answers 4 - 5

4. While you are on patrol, a male, about 21 years old, reports that he had chained his bicycle to a bicycle parking station and gone in to a drugstore to purchase shampoo, only to discover when he came out of the store that his bicycle chain had been cut and his bicycle stolen. You question four witnesses who give you four statements. Which of the following four statements is most likely to be incorrect?

A. The person who cut the chain and rode away with the bicycle was a male, white, about 21 years old and about six feet tall. He was wearing white sneakers, blue dungarees, a yellow T-shirt, and a dark brown backpack. He headed north for one block and then made a left turn.

(MOST LIKELY TO BE INCORRECT. Although the details of this statement agree with most of the other details in the other three statements below, this statement is the only one which describes the sneakers as being "white" instead of "black.")

B. The person who cut the chain was a male, white, about six feet tall. He was wearing <u>black</u> sneakers, blue dungarees, a yellow T-shirt, and a dark brown backpack. He rode the bicycle north for one block and then made a left turn.

C. The person who cut the chain and rode away with the bicycle was a male, white, about six feet tall. He was wearing <u>black</u> sneakers, blue dungarees, a yellow T-shirt, and a dark brown backpack. He pedaled north for one block and then made a left turn.

D. The person who cut the chain and rode away with the bicycle was a male, white, about six feet tall. He was wearing <u>black</u> sneakers, blue dungarees, a yellow T-shirt, and a dark brown backpack. He headed north for one block and then made a left turn.

----

5. Four witnesses to a hit and run accident tell Police Officer Tumi that they memorized the license plate of the car that sped away from the accident. Which of the following is the most likely to be correct?

A. 9237SFG

Choice "A" is <u>not</u> the most likely to be correct because the second numeral "2" differs from the "5" of the other three choices.

B. 9587SFG

Choice "B" is also <u>not</u> the most likely to be correct because the third numeral "8" differs from the "3" of the other three choices.

C. 9537SFG

(Choice "C" is the most likely to be correct. This is the plate number whose numerals agree with most other plate numbers.)

D. 9531SFG

Choice "D" is also <u>not</u> the most likely to be correct because the fourth numeral "1" differs from the "7" of the other three choices.**)**

Question 6

Answer question 6 based on the following table:

Summonses and Desk Appearance Tickets Issued by Police Officer Rinder

Week	Dates	Parking Summonses	Moving Summonses	Desk Appearance Tickets
1	June 1 – 7	24	11	4
2	June 8 - 14	21	8	7
3	June 15 – 21	26	12	2
4	June 22 – 28	19	9	6
5	June 29 – July 5	28	13	9

6. Police Officer Rinder is adding up the total number of summonses and desk appearance tickets issued by her during the above five-week period. Which of the following four formulas should she use to arrive at the correct total of summonses and desk appearance tickets that she issued?

A. 24+21+26+19+28

B. 28 + 13 + 9

C. 24+11+4+21+8+7+26+12+2+19+9+6+28+13+9

D. 1(24+11+4) + 2(21+8+7) + 3(26+12+2) + 4(19+9+6) + 5(28+13+9)

Answer 6

A. 24+21+26+19+28

(NOT CORRECT. This only includes "Parking Summonses" and does not include "Moving Summonses" and "Desk Appearance Tickets.")

B. 28 + 13 + 9

(NOT CORRECT. This only includes summonses and Desk Appearance Tickets issued during the fifth week, June 29 – July 5).

C. 24+11+4+21+8+7+26+12+2+19+9+6+28+13+9 (Total is 199.)

(CORRECT. This includes all the summonses and Desk Appearance Tickets issued during the entire five weeks.)

D. 1(24+11+4) + 2(21+8+7) + 3(26+12+2) + 4(19+9+6) + 5(28+13+9)

(NOT CORRECT. This mathematical formula would give a result of 617.)

INFORMATION ORDERING

9

These questions evaluate your ability to put in order given rules or actions. The rules or actions can include letters, words, sentences, procedures, pictures, and logical or mathematical operations.

The key to answering this type of question correctly is to make sure that the directions are clear to you.

To obtain maximum clarity, take the time to understand the logical order of the directions. Steps that must be done "before" or "after" or "at the same time" should be noted.

Also, at the time of selecting your answer, refer back to the directions to make sure that you have not mentally mixed up the order or the details of the directions.

Question 1

Answer question 1 based on the following "Bomb Threat Procedure."

Bomb Threat Procedure

Some bomb threats are received by phone. A Police Officer who receives a bomb threat by phone should do the following in the order specified:

1. Stay calm. Do not hang up, even if the caller hangs up. Be polite and show interest in what the caller is saying.

2. If possible, write a message to a fellow officer or other Police Department employee.

3. If your phone displays the caller number, write down the number.

4. Even if the caller hangs up, do not hang up your phone. Use a different phone that is not a cell phone to contact the "Bomb Threat Notification Unit."

5. As soon as possible, complete the "Bomb Threat Checklist."

-----

1. At a "Bomb Threat Exercise" conducted at the precinct, you are told that you have answered a phone call during which a bomb threat is made. You have written a note and notified a Police Officer working at the desk next to yours. You have also written down the caller's number which displayed on your phone unit. The caller hangs up. The next step you should take is to:

A. Hang up the phone and immediately call the "Bomb Threat Notification Unit."

B. Do not hang up the phone, but use a cell phone to contact the "Bomb Threat Notification Unit."

C. Complete the form "Bomb Threat Checklist."

D. Do not hang up and use a different phone (not a cell phone) to contact the "Bomb Threat Notification Unit."

Answer 1

Answer question 1 based on the following "Bomb Threat Procedure."

Bomb Threat Procedure

Some bomb threats are received by phone. A Police Officer who receives a bomb threat by phone should do the following in the order specified:

> 1. Stay calm. Do not hang up, even if the caller hangs up. Be polite and show interest in what the caller is saying.

> 2. If possible, write a message to a fellow officer or other Police Department employee.

> 3. If your phone displays the caller number, write down the number.

> 4. Even if the caller hangs up, <u>do not hang up your phone. Use a different phone that is not a cell phone</u> to contact the "Bomb Threat Notification Unit."

> 5. As soon as possible, complete the "Bomb Threat Checklist."

-----

1. At a "Bomb Threat Exercise" conducted at the precinct, you are told that you have answered a phone call during which a bomb threat is made. You have written a note and notified a Police Officer working at the desk next to yours. You have also written down the caller's number which displayed on your phone unit. The caller hangs up. The next step you should take is to:

A. Hang up the phone and immediately call the "Bomb Threat Notification Unit."
(WRONG. Number 1 states, "Do <u>not</u> hang up...")

B. Do not hang up the phone, but use a cell phone to contact the "Bomb Threat Notification Unit."
(WRONG. Number 3 states, "Use a different phone that is <u>not</u> a cell phone...")

C. Complete the form "Bomb Threat Checklist."

(WRONG. Number 5 states, "complete the form "Bomb Threat Checklist." This is the last step and is done after contacting the "Bomb Threat Notification Unit.")

D. Do not hang up and use a different phone (not a cell phone) to contact the "Bomb Threat Notification Unit."
(CORRECT. This is step number four and comes directly after step number three, "...write down the number," which you have already done.)

Information Ordering Question 2

Answer question 2 based on the following "Abandoned Vehicle Procedure."

Police Officer Palenco receives the following new "Abandoned Vehicle Procedure."

Abandoned Vehicle Procedure

1. An abandoned vehicle must be reported to Police Dispatch at 718-555-0105.

2. A police officer will be assigned to attach a notice on the vehicle instructing the owner to remove the vehicle within 48 hours.

3. If the vehicle is not removed within 72 hours, the same officer who reported the abandoned vehicle will complete an AVR (Abandoned Vehicle Information) form and submit it to the precinct (VR Office).

4. The VR office will assign the report an incident report number and e-mail it to the city Department of Environmental Hazards.

5. If the vehicle is not removed within 48 hours, the Department of Environmental Hazards will tow the vehicle to the Waste Metal Recovery Site located in the borough.

-----

2. Officer Palenco is informed by an angry shop owner that a vehicle has been parked in front of his store for the past 3 months without it ever being moved and has accumulated 22 parking tickets. According to the Abandoned Vehicle Procedure, Officer Polanco should:

A. Complete an AVR report and submit it to the precinct (VR Office), as three months have already passed and the shop owner is angry.

B. He should attach a notice on the vehicle instructing the owner to remove the vehicle within 48 hours.

C. Report the abandoned vehicle to Police Dispatch by informing his sergeant, as this will speed up the process.

D. Report the abandoned vehicle to Police Dispatch at 718-555-0105.

Answer 2

Answer question 2 based on the following "Abandoned Vehicle Procedure."

Police Officer Palenco receives the following new "Abandoned Vehicle Procedure."

Abandoned Vehicle Procedure

1. An abandoned vehicle must be reported to Police Dispatch at 718-555-0105.

2. A police officer will be assigned to attach a notice on the vehicle instructing the owner to remove the vehicle within 48 hours.

3. If the vehicle is not removed within 72 hours, the same officer who reported the abandoned vehicle will complete an AVR (Abandoned Vehicle Information) form and submit it to the precinct (VR Office).

4. The VR office will assign the report an incident report number and e-mail it to the city Department of Environmental Hazards.

5. If the vehicle is not removed within 48 hours, the Department of Environmental Hazards will tow the vehicle to the Waste Metal Recovery Site located in the borough.

2. Officer Palenco is informed by an angry shop owner that a vehicle has been parked in front of his store for the past 3 months without it ever being moved and has accumulated 22 parking tickets. According to the Abandoned Vehicle Procedure, Officer Palenco should:

A. Complete an AVR report and submit it to the precinct (VR Office), as three months have already passed and the shop owner is angry.

(WRONG: The first thing he must do is report the abandoned vehicle to Police Dispatch at 718-555-0105.)

B. He should attach a notice on the vehicle instructing the owner to remove the vehicle within 48 hours.

(WRONG. <u>After</u> Police Officer Palenco reports the abandoned vehicle, "A police officer will be assigned to attach a notice on the vehicle instructing the owner to remove the vehicle within 48 hours.")

C. Report the abandoned vehicle to Police Dispatch by informing his sergeant, as this will speed up the process.

(WRONG. The report must be done by telephone and not to his sergeant. There are no steps in the procedure to "speed up the process.")

D. Report the abandoned vehicle to Police Dispatch at 718-555-0105.

(CORRECT. Regardless of how long the vehicle has been there or how angry the shop owner is, the correct first step is to report the abandoned vehicle to Police Dispatch.)

Information Ordering Question 3

Your supervisor gives you five "Complaint Forms" with the following priority numbers:

2867   19643   0344   783   8249

He asks you to organize the forms in ascending priority.

3. According to the above, the third Complaint Form would be Complaint Form number:

A. 8249

B. 2867

C. 783

D. 0344

Answer 3

Examples of <u>ascending order</u> and <u>descending order</u>

Ascending Priority Number Order	Descending Priority Number Order
1	5
2	4
3	3
4	2
5	1

The Complaint Forms in Ascending Priority Number Order are as follows:

1) 0344

2) 783

3) 2867

4) 8249

5) 19643

The third complaint number on the list is 2867, therefore the correct answer is **B) 2867**.

Question 4

Your supervisor gives you five "Requests for Investigation" forms submitted by residents in your precinct. The forms were submitted by the following five persons:

George Felder, Harriet Volker, Ben Halston, Abe Johnson, Diane Molton

He asks you to organize the forms in last name alphabetical order.

4. According to the above, the fourth "Request for Investigation" form is the one submitted by:

A. Halston, Ben

B. Volker, Harriet

C. Molton, Diane

D. Felder, George

Answer 4

The correct listing in last name alphabetical order is:

1) Felder, George

2) Halston, Ben

3) Johnson, Abe

4) Molton, Diane

5) Volker, Harriet

The fourth name on the list is Molton, Diane, therefore the correct answer is **C) Molton, Diane**.

Question 5

5. The ninth letter of the alphabet is:

A) H

B) J

C) I

D. G

Answer 5

The letters of the alphabet (in order) are as follows:

A,   B,   C,   D,   E,   F,   G,   H,   **I**   J,   K,   L   M.....

1........2........3........4.......5........6.........7........8.........**9**........10.......11.......12.......13....

The correct answer is **C) I.**

Question 6

6. You are assigned to drive the precinct van. Your sergeant asks you to make five stops to pick up police officers. At the first two stops you are to pick up six police officers at each stop.

At the last three stops you are to pick up four police officers at each stop. Which of the following mathematical expressions correctly states the total number of police officers that you will pick up at the five stops?

A) 2 + 6 + 3 + 4   B) 2 X 6 X 3 X 4   C) 2 + 3   D) 2(6) + 3(4)

Answer 6

At the first two stops you will pick up six police officers at each stop (6 + 6 = 12 police officers). At the last three stops you will pick up 4 police officers at each stop (4 + 4 + 4 = 12 police officers). The total number of police officers to be picked up is therefore 24 (because 12 + 12 = 24 police officers).

The A, B, C, and D choices would yield the following results:

A) 2 + 6 + 3 + 4 (This gives a total of 15).

B) 2 X 6 X 3 X 4 (This gives a total of 144.)

C) 2 + 3 (This gives a total of 5.)

D) 2(6) + 3(4) = 24

(The mathematical expression 2(6) + 3(4) means (2 X 6) + (3 X 4) = 24. The correct answer therefore is **D) 2(6) + 3(4)**.)

Question 7

Organize the following four sentences in the best logical order:

1. This training includes classroom and "on the street" practice driving.

2. Because of this, they receive proper driving and safety instruction.

3. "On the street" driving is stressed and comprises eighty percent of the training time.

4. Police Officers may be assigned to drive a precinct van.

(A) 1, 3, 4, 2   (B) 2, 3, 4, 1   (C) 3, 2, 1, 4   (D) 4, 2, 1, 3

Answer 7

The correct answer is **(D) 4, 2, 1, 3.**

4. Police Officers may be assigned to drive a precinct van. (This sentence introduces the topic of driving a precinct van.)

2. Because of this, they receive proper driving and safety instruction.

1. This training includes classroom and "on the street" practice driving.

3. "On the street" driving is stressed and comprises eighty percent of the training time.

(After sentence 4, sentences 2, 1, and 3 follow logically in that order.)

Question 8

Your sergeant hands you five "Overtime Request Forms" which you submitted for processing. He reminds you that all overtime requests must be submitted in date order and numbered sequentially. The dates on the overtime forms are as follows:

10-4-2016   9/24/2016   October 1, 2016   September 28, 2016   Sept. 12, 2016

He asks you to number the forms in ascending date order and that you resubmit them.

Assuming that you organize the forms as your supervisor asks and that you number the first request "Request 1," which of the above dated requests would be numbered "Request 3"?

A. 10-4-2016

B. 9/24/2016

C. October 1, 2016

D. September 28, 2016

Answer 8

The correct ascending date order is:

1) Sept. 12, 2016

2) 9/24/2016

3) September 28, 2016

4) October 1, 2016

5) 10-4-2016

The third date on the list is September 28, 2016. Therefore, the correct answer is
D). September 28, 2016.

Question 9

The following are four sentences. Each sentence (listed in random order) is one of the four steps necessary to attach a metal shield to the front of a van. Which one of the following choices (A, B, C, D) lists the order of sentences which best expresses the logical sequence of metal shield installation?

   1. Drive the van slowly forward to test whether the shield is securely bolted to the van.

   2. Tighten the bolts with heavy duty nuts.

   3. Align the front of the van with the shield connectors.

   4. Insert connecting bolts in aligned holes of shield and the van's shield connectors.

A. 1, 4, 2, 3

B. 2, 3, 4, 1

C. 4, 1, 3, 2

D. 3, 4, 2, 1

Answer 9

The correct answer is **D. 3, 4, 2, 1.** (In this order, the sentences are logically connected.)

3. Align the front of the van with the shield connectors.

4. Insert connecting bolts in aligned holes of shield and the van's shield connector.

2. Tighten the bolts with heavy duty nuts.

1. Drive the van slowly forward to test whether the shield is securely bolted to the van.

"Successful and unsuccessful people do not vary greatly in their abilities. They vary in their desires to reach their potential."

– John Maxwell

SPATIAL ORIENTATION

10

These questions evaluate your ability to determine your location and the location of an object with respect to you.

For this type of question, try to keep in mind the following North-East-South-West directional diagram.

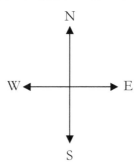

As you read the directional information provided, draw the route (as shown in the answers provided for these types of questions.)

Example: The car travelled east, then south, then west:

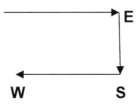

FLORIDA LAW ENFORCEMENT BASIC ABILITIES TEST (BAT) EXAM GUIDE

1. You and another officer notice an elderly man laying down on the street and bleeding from his right arm. He tells you that a large dog that was frothing at the mouth just bit him. You notice the dog running down the block northbound to the end of the block where he makes a right turn. While your partner stays with the victim, you follow the dog and observe him continuing to run for two blocks before turning right.

According to the information in the preceding passage, you would be most correct to radio that you last saw the dog running:

A) north   B) south   C) east   D) west

-----

2. While in your patrol car, you notice a car with what seems to be a teenage driver sideswipe a parked car and then drive off southbound without stopping. You follow the car, which after six blocks makes a right turn and then after two more blocks makes a left turn.

According to the information in the preceding passage, you would be most correct to radio that you last saw the car heading:

A) north   B) south   C) east   D) west

-----

3. Your attention is drawn to a shopkeeper shouting "He robbed me!" and pointing to a man running down the block. You shout for the man to stop, but he continues running eastbound. After three blocks, he makes a right turn and runs for two more blocks before making another right turn.

According to the information in the preceding passage, you would be most correct to radio that you last saw the man heading:

A) north   B) south   C) east   D) west

Answers 1 – 3

1. You and another officer notice an elderly man laying down on the street and bleeding from his right arm. He tells you that a large dog that was frothing at the mouth just bit him. You notice the dog running down the block northbound to the end of the block where he makes a right turn. While your partner stays with the victim, you follow the dog and observe him continuing to run for two blocks before turning right.

According to the information in the preceding passage, you would be most correct to radio that you last saw the dog running:

A) north   **B) south**

C) east   D) west

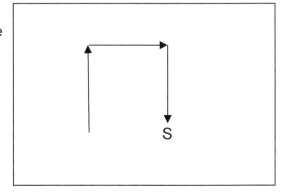

-----

2. While in your patrol car, you notice a car with what seems to be a teenage driver sideswipe a parked car and then drive off southbound without stopping. You follow the car, which after six blocks makes a right turn and then after two more blocks makes a left turn.

According to the information in the preceding passage, you would be most correct to radio that you last saw the car heading:

A) north   **B) south**

C) east   D) west

-----

3. Your attention is drawn to a shopkeeper shouting, "He robbed me!" and pointing to a man running down the block. You shout for the man to stop, but he continues running eastbound. After three blocks, he makes a right turn and runs for two more blocks before making another right turn.

According to the information in the preceding passage, you would be most correct to radio that you last saw the man heading:

A) north   B) south

C) east   **D) west**

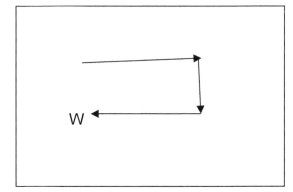

Questions 4 – 6

4. You and another officer witness a masked man snatch a purse from an elderly woman in front of a department store. You shout for the man to stop, but he runs down the block in an eastbound direction. You chase the man for two blocks before he turns right and then runs for another block, at which point he turns left.

According to the information in the preceding passage, you would be most correct to radio that the man was running:

A) north   B) south   C) east   D) west

-----

5. While in your patrol car, you witness two men run out of a bank, both holding a pouch and a revolver. They quickly get into a car and head southbound. You follow. After three six blocks, they make a right turn and then after two more blocks they make another right turn.

According to the information in the preceding passage, you would be most correct to radio that you last saw the car heading:

A) north   B) south   C) east   D) west

-----

6. Your attention is drawn to a pedestrian shouting, "He just ran over me with his bike!" and pointing to a man on a bike pedaling quickly on the sidewalk, away from the pedestrian and in an eastbound direction. After three blocks, he makes a right turn and runs for two more blocks before making another right turn.

According to the information in the preceding passage, you would be most correct to radio that you last saw the man heading:

A) north   B) south   C) east   D) west

Spatial Orientation Answers 4 - 6

4. You and another officer witness a masked man snatch a purse from an elderly woman in front of a department store. You shout for the man to stop, but he runs down the block in an eastbound direction. You chase the man for two blocks before he turns right and then runs for another block, at which point he turns left.

According to the information in the preceding passage, you would be most correct to radio that the man was running:

A) north   B) south

C) east   D) west

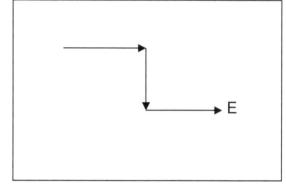

-----

5. While in your patrol car, you witness two men run out of a bank, both holding a pouch and a revolver. They quickly get into a car and head southbound. You follow. After three six blocks, they make a right turn and then after two more blocks they make another right turn.

According to the information in the preceding passage, you would be most correct to radio that you last saw the car heading:

A) north   B) south

C) east   D) west

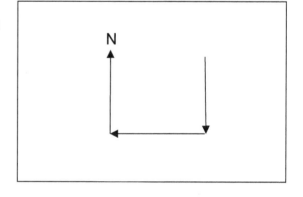

-----

6. Your attention is drawn to a pedestrian shouting, "He just ran over me with his bike!" and pointing to a man on a bike pedaling quickly on the sidewalk, away from the pedestrian and in an eastbound direction. After three blocks, he makes a right turn and runs for two more blocks before making another right turn.

According to the information in the preceding passage, you would be most correct to radio that you last saw the man heading:

A) north   B) south

C) east   **D) west**

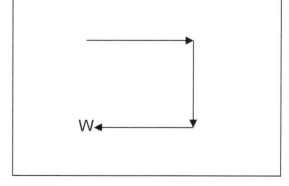

VISUALIZATION

11

These questions evaluate your ability to understand how an object would look when it is rotated or unfolded, moved or changed in any manner.

When you examine images that are changed:

1. Look for differences among the images.

2. Cosmetic differences on faces or objects (lipstick, eye shadow, etc., do not make it a different face or object).

When you examine images that are moved or rotated:

1. Try to form a strong mental image of the way it looks originally.

2. Note any distinguishing facts, points, sections, or patterns.

3. Compare carefully the features you have noted in the original image to each of the image choices provided.

Question 1

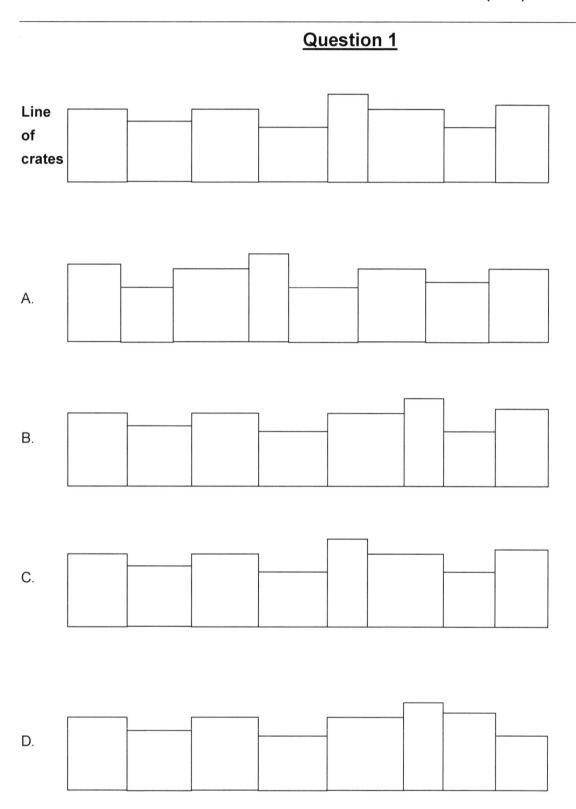

1. Officer Rodriguez is searching for a suspect hiding in a warehouse. He passes a "Line of crates" from the front of the crates. He hears a creek, but keeps walking. A minute later (when he is several rows behind these crates) he decides to return and investigate. How would the "Line of crates" appear as viewed from the back? (A, B, C, or D?)

Questions 2 - 5

Read the following passage, then answer questions 2 - 5 based on the information contained in the passage.

While on patrol, Police Officers Colandro and Feinstein are dispatched to 2834 Boylan Avenue, first floor, "Supreme Arts and Crafts, Inc." at 9:22 p.m. on September 27, 2016. The owner of "Supreme Arts and Crafts, Inc." had just called 911 to report a burglary. They arrive at the store at 9:24 p.m. and are greeted by Mr. Howard Garmen, the owner of the store and Mr. Felix Cuedo, an employee of "Supreme Arts and Crafts, Inc."

Mr. Garmen tells the officers that he and Felix Cuedo had closed the store for the day at 7:00 p.m. They had locked the front and back doors and properly rolled down the security gate and padlocked it. Mr. Garmen discovered the burglary at 9:01 p.m. when at home he happened to glance at the live video of his four security cameras. Although security camera #1 showed the outdoor front entrance and security camera #4 showed the outdoor back door area, it was with security cameras #2 and #3 that he saw the burglars. Security camera #2 covered the outdoor roof skylight and security camera #3 covered the inside area of the store, including the cashier area.

Two burglars, all dressed in black and wearing black face masks, had broken the glass in the skylight and with a rope had descended into the store. The smaller of the two persons descended first and the much taller one followed. The person who descended first carried a black garbage bag and the other person held a flashlight in his right hand.

The two burglars took all the $125.00 cash and coins that had been left in the cash register, a box of collectible statuettes worth $1500.00, three expensive brushes and paints sets worth a total of $900.00, two electric easels worth $179 each, and six original signed watercolor paintings by a local artist worth $129.00 each. Mr. Garmen tells the officers that he will prepare a complete list of missing items as soon as possible.

Mr. Garmen tells Officer Feinstein that he is 58 years old and lives at 2869 Batchelder Avenue in Miami. His cell number is 718-555-2987. Felix Cuedo tells Officer Feinstein that he is 29 years old and lives at 3845 East 289 Street, Miami. His cell number is 718-555-3991.

Police Officers Colandro and Feinstein complete their investigation at 10:05 p.m. Before they completed their crime report, they performed a careful sweep of the store to make sure that the burglars had left.

-----

2. Which of the following security cameras cover the outdoor areas?

A. 1 and 2 only

B. 1, 2, 3, and 4

C. 1, 2, and 4 only

D. 1, 2, and 3 only

----

3. Which of the following statements is correct?

A. The taller man carried a black garbage bag and the smaller man held a flashlight in his right hand.

B. The two burglars were dressed all in grey.

C. The taller person descended first and carried a flashlight in his right hand.

D. The shorter person carried a black garbage bag and the taller person held a flashlight in his right hand.

----

4. Which one of the following statements is correct? Among the items stolen were:

A. three expensive brushes and paints sets worth $900.00 each.

B. two electric easels worth a total of $179.

C. $725.00 cash and coins that had been left in the cash register.

D. six original signed watercolor paintings by a local artist worth a total of $774.00.

----

5. Which of the following statements is correct according to the information provided by Mr. Garmen and Mr. Felix Cuedo?

A. Felix Cuedo tells Officer Feinstein that he is 29 years old and lives at 3845 East 298 Street, Miami. His cell number is 718-555-3991.

B. Mr. Garmen tells Officer Feinstein that he is 58 years old and lives at 2896 Batchelder Avenue in Miami. His cell number is 718-555-2987.

C. Felix Cuedo tells Officer Feinstein that his cell number is 718-555-2987.

D. Mr. Garmen tells Officer Feinstein that he lives at 2869 Batchelder Avenue in Miami.

Answer 1

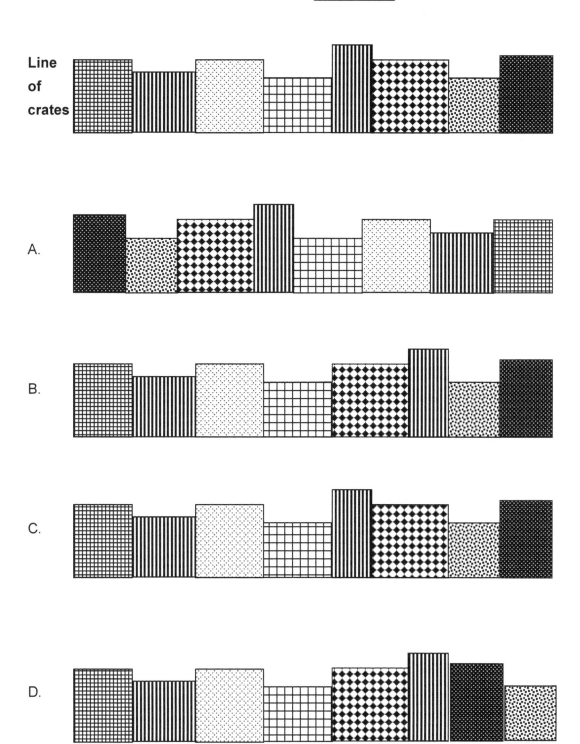

1. The answer is "A."

(To make the answer obvious, we have filled in each corresponding box with the same pattern.)

Visualization Answers 2 – 5

2. Which of the following security cameras cover the outdoor areas?

A. 1 and 2 only

B. 1, 2, 3, and 4

C. 1, 2, and 4 only

("...security camera #3 covered the inside area of the store, including the cashier area.")

D. 1, 2, and 3 only

----

3. Which of the following statements is correct?

A. The taller man carried a black garbage bag and the smaller man held a flashlight in his right hand.

(WRONG. The smaller of the two persons descended first and the much taller one followed. The person who descended first carried a black garbage bag and the other person held a flashlight in his right hand.)

B. The two burglars were dressed all in grey.

(WRONG. "The two burglars, all dressed in <u>black</u> and wearing black face masks...)

C. The taller person descended first and carried a flashlight in his right hand.

(WRONG. The <u>smaller</u> of the two persons descended first.)

D. The shorter person carried a black garbage bag and the taller person held a flashlight in the right hand.

(CORRECT. "The smaller of the two persons descended first and the much taller one followed. The person who descended first carried a black garbage bag and the other person held a flashlight in the right hand.")

----

4. Which one of the following statements is correct? Among the items stolen were:

A. three expensive brushes and paints sets worth $900.00 each.

(WRONG. The tree sets <u>totaled</u> $900.00.)

B. two electric easels worth a total of $179.

(WRONG. <u>Each</u> easel is worth $179.)

C. $725.00 cash and coins that had been left in the cash register.

(WRONG. The correct amount of cash and coins is $125.)

D. <u>six original signed watercolor paintings by a local artist worth a total of $774.00.</u>

(CORRECT. "$129.00 each X 6 = $774.00)

----

5. Which of the following statements is correct according to the information provided by Mr. Garmen and Mr. Felix Cuedo?

A. Felix Cuedo tells Officer Feinstein that he is 29 years old and lives at 3845 East 298 Street, Miami. His cell number is 555-3991.

(WRONG. Felix Cuedo lives at East <u>289</u> Street.)

B. Mr. Garmen tells Officer Feinstein that he is 58 years old and lives at 2896 Batchelder Avenue in Miami. His cell number is 718-555-2987.

(WRONG. The correct street address is <u>2869</u> Batchelder Avenue.)

C. Felix Cuedo tells Officer Feinstein that his cell number is 718-555-2987.

(WRONG. The correct cell number is <u>718-555-3991</u>.)

D. <u>Mr. Garmen tells Officer Feinstein that he lives at 2869 Batchelder Avenue in Miami.</u>

(CORRECT. "Mr. Garmen tells Officer Feinstein that he is 58 years old and lives at 2869 Batchelder Avenue in Miami.")

> "Focused, hard work is the key to success."
>
> — John Carmack

Visualization Question 6

During her patrol, Police Officer Dawn Heller is called to the scene of an accident. The driver/owner of vehicle #3 stated that he was driving on Vine St. and making a right turn to Hart Avenue when car #1 hit his car from behind, causing him to hit vehicle #2.

Assume that all 3 vehicles were in their proper lanes of traffic.

Which of the following four diagrams best matches the statement of the driver of vehicle #3?

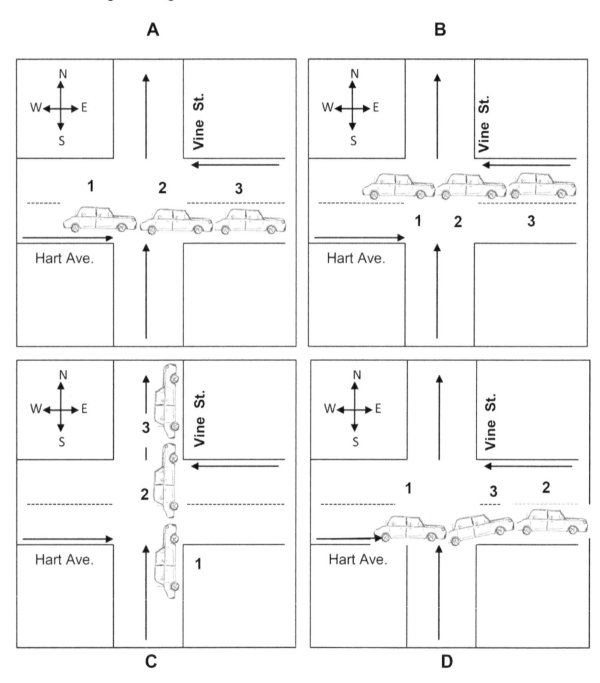

6. The diagram which best matches the statement of driver of vehicle #3 is:
A. diagram "A"   C. diagram "C"
C. diagram "B"   D. diagram "D"

Answer 6

6. The diagram which best matches the statement of driver of vehicle #3 is:

A. diagram "A"

B. diagram "B"

C. diagram "C"

D. diagram "D" (Answer)

Why?

According to the question, "The driver/owner of vehicle #3 stated that he was driving on Vine St. and making a right turn when car #1 hit his car from behind, causing him to hit vehicle number 2."

"Car 1 hits Car 3 which hits Car 2"

1 > 3 > 2

The only choice which displays the collision in this sequence <u>and in the proper lane</u> is choice **"D."**

Questions 7 - 9

Answer question 7 based on the following information.

Officer Lagnier collects the following information at the scene of an auto accident:

Date of Accident: August 16, 2016

Time of accident: 5:02 p.m.

Place of accident: intersection of Ferndale Avenue and Willows Avenue, Hollywood

Driver: Alfred Kearns

Vehicle: 2007 Toyota Sienna

Damage: Vehicle struck a bicycle partially parked on the sidewalk, but protruding into the street.

-----

7. Officer Lagnier is preparing a report of the accident and has four drafts of the report. He wishes to use the draft that expresses the information most clearly, accurately and completely. Which draft should he choose?

A. At 5:02 p.m., on August 16, 2016, at the intersection of Ferndale Avenue and Willows Avenue, Hollywood, a vehicle driven by Alfred Kearns struck a bicycle partially parked on the sidewalk, but protruding into the street.

B. On August 16, 2016, at 5:02 p.m., at the intersection of Ferndale Avenue and Willows Avenue, Hollywood, a 2007 Toyota Sienna driven by Alfred Karns struck a bicycle partially parked on the sidewalk, but protruding into the street.

C. On August 16, 2016, at 5:02 p.m., at the intersection of Ferndale Avenue and Willows Avenue, Hollywood, a 2007 Toyota Sienna driven by Alfred Kearns struck a bicycle partially parked on the sidewalk, but protruding into the street.

D. At the intersection of Ferndale Avenue and Willows Avenue, Hollywood, on August 16, 2016, at 2:05 p.m., a 2007 Toyota Sienna driven by Alfred Kearns struck a bicycle partially parked on the sidewalk, but protruding into the street.

Answer question 8 based on the following information.

Officer Pintkin responds to a car theft. She questions the owner of the vehicle who reported the car stolen and obtains the following information:

Suspect: Unidentified

Date of crime: August 15, 2016

Time of crime: between 6:20 p.m. and 11:30 p.m.

Crime: theft of car

Vehicle stolen: 2012 Nissan

Victim: owner of car, Lance Bedford

Place of crime: driveway in front of 167 28th Street, Margate

-----

8. Officer Pintkin is preparing a report of the theft and has prepared four drafts of the report. She wishes to use the draft that expresses the information most clearly, accurately and completely. Which of the following drafts should she choose?

A. A car theft of a 2012 Nissan happened at the driveway in front of 167 28th Street, Margate where Lance Bedford's car was parked for the night. The alleged thief is unidentified, as the theft happened in the afternoon.

B. On August 15, 2016, between 6:20 p.m. and 11:30 p.m., at the driveway in front of 167 28th Street, Margate, a 2012 Nissan owned by Lance Bedford was stolen by an unidentified suspect.

C. A car was stolen on August 15, 2016, between 6:20 p.m. and 11:30 p.m., at the driveway in front of 167 28th Street, Margate, owned by Lance Bedford. The suspect is unidentified.

D. On August 15, 2016, at the driveway in front of 167 28th Street, Margate, between 6:30 p.m. and 11:30 p.m., a 2012 Nissan owned by Lance Bedford was stolen by an unidentified suspect.

Answer question 9 based on the following procedure.

When a criminal case is pending in the courts, the Police Officer who made the arrest is prohibited from discussing the case with any newspaper, magazine, TV reporters, and all other media. Exceptions to this are when:

1. a Florida court of competent jurisdiction formally orders the Police Officer to discuss one or more particulars of the case.

2. a Florida authorized Department orders such discussion.

3. the Police Officer is subpoenaed to testify before an authorized Florida or federal board.

The officer must in all cases refer all requests for information to the officer's supervisor.

-----

9. Police Officer Janet Peters arrests a person suspected of kidnapping a child who is still missing. The suspect has been indicted and is in jail, waiting for trial. A newspaper reporter, Brian Collins, contacts Officer Janet Peters and asks for information that might help the reporter to investigate the kidnapping and perhaps locate the missing child. Officer Janet Peters should:

A. give assistance to Brian Collins by providing information that might help to locate the missing child.

B. give assistance only if the reporter can guarantee that the child will be found.

C. provide only information relating to locating the child, and not any other information.

D. not provide any information and report the request to her supervisors.

Answers 7 - 9

Answer question 7 based on the following information.

Officer Lagnier collects the following information at the scene of an auto accident:

Date of Accident: August 16, 2016

Time of accident: 5:02 p.m.

Place of accident: intersection of Ferndale Avenue and Willows Avenue, Hollywood

Driver: Alfred Kearns

Vehicle: 2007 Toyota Sienna

Damage: Vehicle struck a bicycle partially parked on the sidewalk, but protruding into the street.

-----

7. Officer Lagnier is preparing a report of the accident and has four drafts of the report. He wishes to use the draft that expresses the information most clearly, accurately and completely. Which draft should he choose?

A. At 5:02 p.m., on August 16, 2016, at the intersection of Ferndale Avenue and Willows Avenue, Hollywood, a vehicle driven by Alfred Kearns struck a bicycle partially parked on the sidewalk, but protruding into the street.

(WRONG. The information is not complete. The type of vehicle, "2007 Toyota Sienna", is not stated.)

B. On August 16, 2016, at 5:02 p.m., at the intersection of Ferndale Avenue and Willows Avenue, Hollywood, a 2007 Toyota Sienna driven by Alfred <u>Karns</u> struck a bicycle partially parked on the sidewalk, but protruding into the street.

(WRONG. The name of the driver, "Kearns," is misspelled "Karns.")

C. On August 16, 2016, at 5:02 p.m., at the intersection of Ferndale Avenue and Willows Avenue, Hollywood, a 2007 Toyota Sienna driven by Alfred Kearns struck a bicycle partially parked on the sidewalk, but protruding into the street.

(CORRECT. The information is accurate and complete.)

D. At the intersection of Ferndale Avenue and Willows Avenue, Hollywood, on August 16, 2016, at <u>2:05 p.m.,</u> a 2007 Toyota Sienna driven by Alfred Kearns struck a bicycle partially parked on the sidewalk, but protruding into the street.

(WRONG. The time of the accident is not correct. The accident occurred at <u>5:02</u> p.m. and not <u>2:05</u> p.m.)

Answer question 8 based on the following information.

Officer Pintkin responds to a car theft. She questions the owner of the vehicle who reported the car stolen and obtains the following information:

Suspect: Unidentified

Date of crime: August 15, 2016

Time of crime: between 6:20 p.m. and 11:30 p.m.

Crime: theft of car

Vehicle stolen: 2012 Nissan

Victim: owner of car, Lance Bedford

Place of crime: driveway in front of 167 28th Street, Margate

-----

8. Officer Pintkin is preparing a report of the theft and has prepared four drafts of the report. She wishes to use the draft that expresses the information most clearly, accurately and completely. Which of the following drafts should she choose?

A. A car theft of a 2012 Nissan happened at the driveway in front of 167 28th Street, Margate where Lance Bedford's car was parked for the night. The alleged thief is unidentified, as the theft happened in the <u>afternoon</u>.

(WRONG. The date of the crime is missing and the time of the crime is missing. Also, the statement that "The alleged thief is unidentified, as the theft happened in the afternoon" is not correct because it occurred in the evening.)

B. On August 15, 2016, between 6:20 p.m. and 11:30 p.m., at the driveway in front of 167 28th Street, Margate, a 2012 Nissan owned by Lance Bedford was stolen by an unidentified suspect.

(CORRECT. The information is accurate and complete.)

C. A car was stolen on August 15, 2016, between 6:20 p.m. and 11:30 p.m., at the driveway in front of 167 28th Street, Margate, owned by Lance Bedford. The suspect is unidentified.

(WRONG. The type of car, "2012 Nissan", is omitted and the statement is clumsy.)

D. On August 15, 2016, at the driveway in front of 167 28th Street, Margate, between 6:30 a.m. and <u>11:30 a.m.,</u> a 2012 Nissan owned by Lance Bedford was stolen by an unidentified suspect.

(WRONG. The time of the crime is wrong. The summary states "a.m." and it should be "<u>p.m.</u>")

Answer question 9 based on the following procedure.

When a criminal case is pending in the courts, the Police Officer who made the arrest is prohibited from discussing the case with any newspaper, magazine, TV reporters, and all other media. Exceptions to this are when:

1. a Florida court of competent jurisdiction formally orders the Police Officer to discuss one or more particulars of the case.

2. a Florida authorized Department orders such discussion.

3. the Police Officer is subpoenaed to testify before an authorized Florida or federal board.

The officer must in all cases refer all requests for information to the officer's supervisor.

-----

9. Police Officer Janet Peters arrests a person suspected of kidnapping a child who is still missing. The suspect has been indicted and is in jail, waiting for trial. A newspaper reporter, Brian Collins, contacts Officer Janet Peters and asks for information that might help the reporter to investigate the kidnapping and perhaps locate the missing child. Officer Janet Peters should:

A. give assistance to Brian Collins by providing information that might help to locate the missing child.

(WRONG. This does not qualify as one of the three exception to the prohibition from discussing the case.)

B. give assistance only if the reporter can guarantee that the child will be found.

(WRONG. This does not qualify as one of the three exception to the prohibition from discussing the case.)

C. provide only information relating to locating the child, and not any other information.

(WRONG. This does not qualify as one of the three exception to the prohibition from discussing the case.)

D. not provide any information and report the request to her supervisors.

(**CORRECT.** All the other choices do not qualify as exceptions. Officer Peters cannot supply information and must "refer all requests for information to the officer's supervisor," as stated in the last sentence.)

———————

"Make use of your time. Let not advantage slip."

- Shakespeare

FLEXIBILITY OF CLOSURE | 12

Flexibility of Closure questions test a candidate's ability to locate something (an object, shape, etc.) that is difficult to see because it is mixed in with a group of other objects or shapes or letters, etc.

_____

How confident are you at answering an "easy" question?

Question: How many letter "h" (total of lowercase and uppercase) are in the following passage?

> In July 592 BC, at the age of 30, Ezekiel describes his calling to be a prophet, by going into great detail about his encounter with God and four living creatures or Cherubim with four wheels that stayed beside the creatures. For the next five years he incessantly prophesied and acted out the destruction of Jerusalem and its temple, which was met with some opposition. However, Ezekiel and his contemporaries like Jeremiah, another prophet who was living in Jerusalem at that time, witnessed the fulfillment of their prophecies when Jerusalem was finally sacked by the Babylonians. The date of the sacking, 587 BC, is confirmed by Babylonian cuneiform records discovered by archeologists. Ezekiel was 50 years old when he began to have visions of a new Temple. He served as a prophet for at least 22 years until, according to Ezekiel, he last experienced an encounter with God in April 570 BC. [Ezekiel 29:17] His time of death has not been recorded.

Answer: There are 42 "h" (total of lowercase and uppercase) in the above passage

One or two **careless** mistakes (and therefore **avoidable**) mistakes on the exam place you lower than other candidates who were careful and did not lose the one or two points.

Same passage with each "h" numbered:

> In July 592 BC, at **the(1)** age of 30, Ezekiel describes **his(2)** calling to be a **prophet(3),** by going into great detail about **his(4)** encounter **with(5)** God and four living creatures or **Cherubim(6) with(7)** four **wheels(8) that(9)** stayed beside **the(10)** creatures. For **the(11)** next five years **he(12)** incessantly **prophesied(13)** and acted out **the(14)** destruction of Jerusalem and its temple, **which(15 & 16)** was met **with(17)** some opposition. **However,(18)** Ezekiel and **his(19)** contemporaries like **Jeremiah,(20) another(21) prophet(22) who(23)** was living in Jerusalem at **that(24)** time, witnessed **the(25)** fulfillment of **their(26) prophecies(27) when(28)** Jerusalem was finally sacked by **the(29)** Babylonians. **The(30)** date of the**(31)** sacking, 587 BC, is confirmed by Babylonian cuneiform records discovered by **archeologists(32).** Ezekiel was 50 years old **when(33) he(34)** began to **have(35)** visions of a new Temple. **He(36)** served as a **prophet(37)** for at least 22 years until, according to Ezekiel, **he(38)** last experienced an encounter **with(39)** God in April 570 BC.[Ezekiel 29:17] **His(40)** time of **death(41) has(42)** not been recorded.

The total number of "h" (total of lowercase and uppercase) in the above passage is 42.

Answer questions 1 and 2 based on the following display of letters.

D	E	U	J	D	Y	M	Z	W	F	U	N	L
C	g	P	a	H	N	E	U	T	G	C	I	H
Z	K	Y	Q	G	E	C	P	V	F	E	Y	U
C	Y	N	U	S	R	L	Z	Q	F	N	M	J
H	J	W	Y	J	A	G	B	H	M	U	T	C
V	E	K	Z	E	Y	I	L	n	H	T	K	M
S	R	H	M	K	O	D	G	B	N	U	E	Z
A	G	V	U	M	Y	V	E	H	N	I	X	S
R	G	B	J	U	G	E	A	Z	B	N	U	Y
H	R	h	Y	E	K	X	D	V	W	Q	Z	N
U	K	F	T	M	B	H	Y	E	G	J	K	X
W	X	G	U	K	M	G	R	H	d	E	T	Y
X	S	R	Y	F	T	R	T	N	U	F	E	H

1. What is the total number of uppercase letter Hs that are in the above display?

A. 8

B. 9

C. 10

D. 11

----

2. What is the total number of uppercase letter Es that are in the above display?

A. 11

B. 12

C. 13

D. 14

Answer questions 3 and 4 based on the following display of numbers.

4	2	8	6	4	9	4	7	0	1	5	2	6
8	2	7	9	3	5	4	8	9	6	5	4	8
3	5	9	6	8	7	0	3	2	4	5	1	7
6	8	6	7	9	3	4	6	5	2	3	8	6
9	1	3	2	6	9	6	3	6	9	6	8	3
5	2	8	0	2	7	8	4	3	2	4	6	5
7	4	9	2	5	8	9	2	3	6	9	1	0
4	7	9	3	4	2	6	7	9	2	8	0	6
5	4	8	2	7	4	9	1	4	3	8	0	4
3	5	7	6	8	3	9	7	0	3	5	7	6
3	7	8	2	0	5	8	4	2	8	9	2	6
2	9	7	8	3	6	2	5	8	6	7	9	2
1	4	9	5	4	7	2	9	1	6	3	9	3

3. What is the total number of 8s that are in the above display of numbers?

A. 17

B. 18

C. 19

D. 20

----

4. What is the total number of 2s that are in the above display of numbers?

A. 19

B. 20

C. 21

D. 22

FLORIDA LAW ENFORCEMENT BASIC ABILITIES TEST (BAT) EXAM GUIDE

Answer questions 5 and 6 based on the following display of letters and numbers.

2	N	U	J	7	Y	M	Z	W	F	U	N	L
C	g	3	a	W	N	8	U	T	5	C	I	W
Z	5	Y	Q	2	J	C	P	V	F	2	Y	U
C	Y	N	U	S	R	L	Z	Q	F	N	3	J
H	J	5	Y	J	A	G	B	H	5	U	T	C
V	E	9	Z	A	Y	I	L	n	H	T	K	M
S	R	H	5	K	O	D	G	B	8	U	K	Z
2	G	V	U	2	Y	8	E	H	N	I	X	S
R	G	5	J	U	G	D	A	Z	B	N	U	Y
T	R	h	8	I	K	X	D	V	W	Q	5	2
5	K	F	T	M	B	H	5	E	G	8	K	X
W	X	G	7	K	M	G	R	7	d	B	T	Y
X	S	R	Y	F	8	R	T	N	3	F	2	3

5. What is the total number of uppercase letter Gs that are in the above display?

A. 7

B. 8

C. 9

D. 10

----

6. What is the total number of number 5s that are in the above display?

A. 7

B. 8

C. 9

D. 10

----

7. Which of the following four shapes (A, B, C or D) is in the rectangle below? (Note: the shape may be of a different size or rotated, but the relative dimensions of the shape are the same).

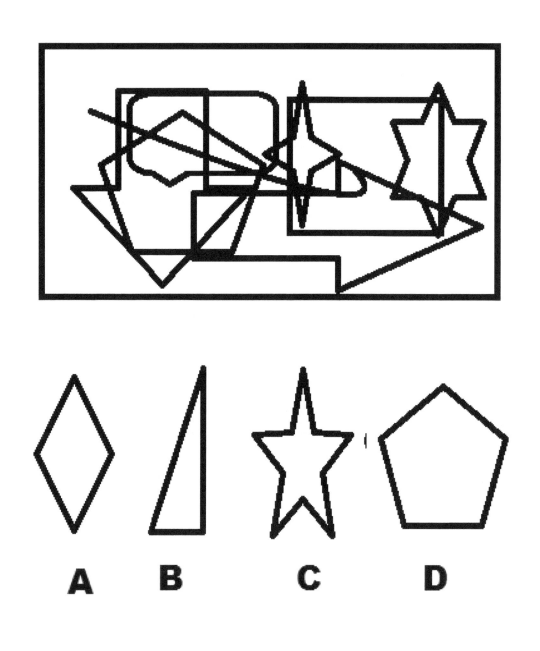

A   **B**   **C**   **D**

8. Which of the following four shapes (A, B, C or D) is in the rectangle below? (Note: the shape may be of a different size or rotated, but the relative dimensions of the shape are the same).

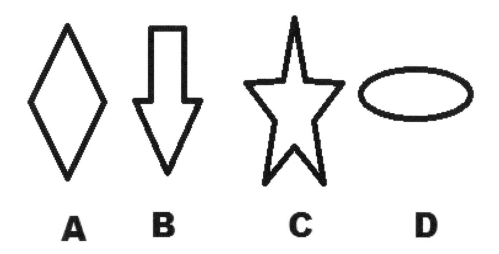

A   **B**   **C**   **D**

Answers for Flexibility of Closure questions 1-8:

1. D. 11	4. C. 21	7. D
2. C. 13	5. B. 8	8. D
3. D. 20	6. C. 9	

SELECTIVE ATTENTION

13

Selective Attention questions test your ability to concentrate on some task without being distracted by things around you or around what you are concentrating on. This skill is important when trying to remember license plate numbers or other numeric or letter information.

Questions

1. Which of the following four choices matches exactly the following Master sequence of numbers, letters, and symbols?

Master sequence: Kæ9T7¥LµÆÆØH9MX//-\4ZTDt¥

A. Kæ9T7¥LµÆÆOH0MX//-\4ZTDt¥

B. Kæ9T7¥LµÆÆØH9MX/-\4ZTDt¥

C. Kæ9T17¥LµÆÆØH9MX//-\4ZTDt¥

D. Kæ9T7¥LµÆÆØH9MX//-\4ZTDt¥

----

2. Which of the following four choices matches exactly the following Master sequence of numbers, letters, and symbols?

Master sequence: X//-\\\4ZTD t¥$€ÆKR8B37¥LµÆÆt¥

A. X//-\\\4ZTD t¥$€ÆKR8B37¥LuÆÆt¥

B. X//-\\\4ZTD t¥$EÆKR8B37¥LµÆÆt¥

C. X//-\\\4ZTD t¥$€ÆKR8B37¥LµÆÆt¥

D. X//-\\\4ZTD t¥$€ÆRR8B37¥LµÆÆt¥

----

3. Which of the following four choices matches the "suspect license plate number?"

Suspect license plate number: 5269-0906*NM

A. 5296-0906*NM

B. 5269-0906*MN

C. 5269-0906*NM

D. 5269-0906*NM

4. Which of the following four choices matches the "suspect license plate number?"

Suspect license plate number: 9625-8371*RK

A. 9625-8317*RK

B. 9652-8371*RK

C. 6925-8371*RK

D. 9625-8371*RK

----

5. Which of the following four choices matches the "suspect home address?"

Suspect home address: 147-291 Ferndale Ave., Miami, FL.

A. 147-291 Ferndate Ave., Miami, FL.

B. 147-921 Ferndale Ave., Miami, FL.

C. 147-291 Fendale Ave., Miami, FL.

D. 147-291 Ferndale Ave., Miami, FL.

----

6. Which of the following four choices matches the "crime scene address?"

Crime scene address: 205271 East Heiker Boulevard, Boca Raton, FL.

A. 205271 East Heiker Buolevard, Boca Raton, FL.

B. 205271 East Hieker Boulevard, Boca Raton, FL.

C. 202571 East Heiker Boulevard, Boca Raton, FL.

D. 205271 East Heiker Boulevard, Boca Raton, FL.

Answers

1. Master sequence: Kæ9T7¥LµÆÆØH9MX//-\4ZTDt¥

    A. Kæ9T7¥LµÆÆ**O**H9MX//-\4ZTDt¥

    B. Kæ9T7¥LµÆÆØH9M**X/**-\4ZTDt¥

    C. Kæ9**T17**¥LµÆÆØH9MX//-\4ZTDt¥

    D. Kæ9T7¥LµÆÆØH9MX//-\4ZTDt¥ (Correct Answer)

----

2. Which of the following four choices matches exactly the following Master sequence of numbers, letters, and symbols?

Master sequence: X//-\\\4ZTD t¥$€ÆKR8B37¥LµÆÆt¥

A. X//-\\\4ZTD t¥$€ÆKR8B37¥L<u>u</u>ÆÆt¥

B. X//-\\\4ZTD t¥<u>$E</u>ÆKR8B37¥LµÆÆt¥

C. X//-\\\4ZTD t¥$€ÆKR8B37¥LµÆÆt¥ (Correct Answer)

D. X//-\\\4ZTD t¥$€Æ<u>RR</u>8B37¥LµÆÆt¥

----

3. Which of the following four choices matches the "suspect license plate number?"
Suspect license plate number: 5269-0906*NM

A. 52<u>96</u>-0906*NM

B. 5269-0906*<u>MN</u>

C. 5269-0906*NM (Correct answer)

D. 5269-0906*NM

----

4. Which of the following four choices matches the "suspect license plate number?"
Suspect license plate number: 9625-8371*RK

A. 9625-83<u>17</u>*RK

B. 96<u>52</u>-8371*RK

C. <u>69</u>25-8371*RK

D. 9625-8371*RK (Correct answer)

----

5. Which of the following four choices matches the "suspect home address?"
Suspect home address: 147-291 Ferndale Ave., Miami, FL.

A. 147-291 Fernd<u>ate</u> Ave., Miami, FL.

B. 147-<u>92</u>1 Ferndale Ave., Miami, FL.

C. 147-291 F<u>end</u>ale Ave., Miami, FL.

D. 147-291 Ferndale Ave., Miami, FL. (Correct answer)

----

6. Which of the following four choices matches the "crime scene address?"
Crime scene address: 205271 East Heiker Boulevard, Boca Raton, FL.

A. 205271 East Heiker B<u>uo</u>levard, Boca Raton, FL.

B. 205271 East Hi<u>e</u>ker Boulevard, Boca Raton, FL.

C. 20<u>25</u>71 East Heiker Boulevard, Boca Raton, FL.

D. 205271 East Heiker Boulevard, Boca Raton, FL. (Correct answer)

PRACTICE TEST QUESTIONS

Memory Question

Study the photo below for the next ten minutes. Try to remember as many details about the people and objects as you can. During the ten minutes, you are not permitted to take any notes or write anything.

At the end of the ten minutes you will be asked to answer questions 1 – 10 (<u>without</u> looking back at the picture.)

(After ten minutes)

Instructions for questions 1 – 10:

<u>Without</u> looking back at the picture, answer questions 1 – 10 on the following page.

1. The number of protestors not wearing any type of mask is:

A. 0   B. 1   C. 2   D. 3

2. How many signboards are displayed in the picture?

A. 6   B. 7   C. 8   D. 9

3. How many people are wearing a white mask?

A. 2   B. 3   C. 4   D. 5

4. The capital letter that appears alone on one of the signs is:

A. "B"   B. "Z"   C. "R"   D. none of the above

5. The two protestors that are holding signs with "USA" and the crossed-out "51" on them:

A. are wearing black shirts.

B. are both wearing white jackets.

C. are of the same height.

D. are wearing black face masks.

6. The dark signboard that is ripped at the corner:

A. has the word "Peace" on it.

B. has the word "NO" on it.

C. has the letters "USA" on it.

D. none of the above

7. How many signs have the letters "USA" on the sign?

A. 1   B. 2   C. 3   D. 4

8. The "smiley face":

A. is on a white background.

B. is being held above the heads of the crowd.

C. is on two signs.

D. does not have a nose.

9. How many signs have a "star" drawn on them?

A. 1   B. 2   C. 3   D. 4

10. How many signs do not have anything written, printed or displayed on them?

A. 0   B. 1   C. 2   D. 3

Questions 11 - 15

Answer questions 11 - 15 based on the information contained in the following paragraphs.

Police Officers Frank Torres and Diane Washington were on patrol on August 13, 2016 when at 9:45 p.m. they witnessed a minor traffic accident (at East 16th Street and Kings Highway in Miami). Officer Torres called the Police Dispatcher at 9:50 p.m. and reported that the two drivers, and two passengers (one in each vehicle) did not sustain any personal injuries. One of the vehicles, the one driven by a male named Felix Upton, did have minor damage to the windshield, and the other vehicle, driven by a male named Mark Levington, had extensive damage to the driver's side front door.

Officer Washington examined the driver's licenses, vehicle registration certificates and vehicle insurance identification cards. The auto driven by Felix Upton, age 46, was a black 2012 Ford Edge, FL. license plate 4357ZB, owned by the driver, residing at 1942 West 58th Street, Miami. Mr. Upton's FL. driver's license identification number is D274 43 662 and the expiration date is December 31, 2018.

The driver of the other auto was Mark Levington, age 52, residing at 2686 Manor Street, Miami. Mr. Levington's auto was a blue 2011 Ford Escape, FL. license plate 607PHB. Mr. Levington's driver's license identification number is A214 295 337 and the expiration is December 31, 2018.

Officers Torres and Washington completed a Vehicle Accident Report at 10:15 p.m. The report number was 48392747332.

-----

11. What is the time of the accident?
A. 9:50 p.m.
B. 10:15 p.m.
C. 9:45 p.m.
D. before 9:30 a.m.

----

12. How many persons were injured because of the traffic accident?
A. 1
B. 0
C. 2
D. none of the above

----

13. Which car sustained extensive damage to the driver's side front door?
A. FL. plate #607PHB, black 2012 Ford Edge
B. FL. plate #4357ZN, black 2012 Ford Edge
C. FL. plate #4357ZN, blue 2011 Ford Escape
D. FL. plate #607PHB, blue 2011 Ford Escape

14. Which of the following statements is not correct?
A. The auto driven by Felix Upton, age 46, was a black 2012 Ford Edge.
B. The vehicle Accident Report number was 4839274732.
C. Mark Levington, age 52, resides at 2686 Manor Street, Miami.
D. Mr. Upton's FL. driver's license identification number is D274 43 662.

----

15. Which of the following is correct?
A. The person residing at 1942 West 58th Street, Miami has a FL. driver's license identification number D274 43 665 with an expiration date of December 31, 2018.
B. Mark Levington, age 25, resides at 2686 Manor Street, Miami.
C. The auto driven by Felix Upton, is a black 2012 Ford Edge, FL. license plate 4357ZB.
D. The accident occurred at East 16th Street and Kings Highway in Marna.

Questions 16 - 20

Answer questions 16 - 20 based on the information contained in the following paragraphs.

Police Officers George Elton and Jasmine Colbert were on patrol in their squad car on September 17, 2016 when at 9:35 p.m. a man approached them. The man pointed to his parked car, a silver Toyota, and stated that the red Ford Taurus parked behind it had just done some damage to the back of his car while the Taurus was parking. Police Officer George Elton called the police dispatcher at 9:40 p.m. and reported the traffic accident, which occurred in front of 924 6th Avenue, Palmetto. Police Officer Jasmine Colbert questioned the driver of the Taurus. Both Police Officers reported to the dispatcher that the driver of the silver Toyota and the driver of the damaged red Ford Taurus did not sustain any injuries. Also, there were no passengers in the two cars. One of the vehicles, the silver Toyota, was driven and owned by a male, Fred Elkinson. It had moderate damage to the back bumper and rear tail lights. The other vehicle, owned by a female, Barbara Baker, sustained no damage.

Officer Elton examined the driver's licenses, vehicle registration certificates and vehicle insurance identification cards. The auto driven by Fred Elkinson, age 51, was a 2008 silver Toyota, FL. license plate 36823EL, owned by the driver, residing at 62 West Garry Road, Palmetto. Mr. Elkinson's FL. driver's license identification number is R3241 35532 32578 and the expiration date is October 31, 2018.

The owner of the Taurus was Barbara Baker, age 46, residing at 234 West 9th Street, Palmetto Ms. Baker's auto was a 2009 red Ford Taurus, FL. license plate KB3463H. Ms. Baker's driver's license identification number is D413 742 533 and the expiration is November 30, 2018. Officers Elton and Colbert completed a Vehicle Accident Report at 9:50 p.m.
The report number was 224376654522.

-----

16. Select the best answer: The time closest to the time of the accident is:
A. 9:35 a.m.   C. 9:40 p.m.
B. 6:50 p.m.   D. 9:35 p.m.

----

17. Which car sustained damage to the rear bumper and rear tail lights?
A.   FL. plate #36823EL, red Ford Taurus
B.   FL. plate #3463HKB, silver 2008 Toyota
C.   FL. plate #36823EL, silver 2008 Toyota
D.   FL. plate #3463HKB, red Ford Taurus

----

18. At what time was the Vehicle Accident Report completed?
A. 9:35 p.m.   B. 9:40 p.m.   C. 9:50 p.m.   D. 9:55 p.m.

----

19. Which of the following statements is correct?
A. The license plate number of the car owned by Barbara Baker is KD3463H.
B. The report number is 224376654522.
C. Police Officer Jasmine Colbert called the police dispatcher at 9:40 p.m.
D. The vehicle driven and owned by Fred Elkinson had moderate damage to the front bumper and rear tail lights.

----

20. Which of the following statements is correct?
A. Police Officer Jasmine Colbert questioned the driver of the Toyota.
B. Barbara Baker is 64 years old.
C. Officers Elton and Colbert completed a Vehicle Accident Report at 9:05 p.m.
D. Mr. Fred Elkinson's FL. driver's license identification number is R3241 35532 32578.

_____

Questions 21 - 26

Answer questions 21 - 26 based on the information contained in the following paragraphs.

Police Officers David Alberts and Carol Sumpter were on patrol in their squad car on August 23, 2016 when at 8:25 p.m. a female approached them. The female stated that she had just been involved in a car accident with the black Honda that was now stopped next to her car, a red Ford. Police Officer David Alberts called the police dispatcher at 8:33 p.m. and reported the traffic accident (which occurred in front of 1976 East 17th Street, Sanford). Police Officer Carol Sumpter questioned the driver of the black Honda. Both Police Officers reported to the dispatcher that both drivers did not sustain any injuries. Also, there were no passengers in the two cars. One of the vehicles, the red Ford, was driven and owned by a female, Nancy Wright. It had damage to the rear bumper. The other vehicle, driven by a female, Tania Salters, had damage to the front bumper.

Officer Alberts examined the driver's licenses, vehicle registration certificates and vehicle insurance cards. The auto driven by Nancy Wright, age 38, was a red 2006 Ford, FL. license plate 35434DE, owned by the driver, residing at 304 West Almeria Road, Sanford. Ms. Wright's FL. driver's license identification number is W3547 28592 12332 and the expiration date is September 30, 2018.

The driver and owner of the other auto was Tania Salters, age 26, residing at 183 Madison Street, Sanford, FL. Ms. Salters' auto was a 2007 black Honda, FL. license plate 4492GDX. Ms. Salters' driver's license identification number is H215 594 732 and the expiration is November 30, 2018.

Officers Alberts and Sumpter completed a Vehicle Accident Report at 8:40 p.m. The report number was 224376754321.

-----

21. Select the best answer. The closest time of the accident is approximately:
A. after 8:35 p.m.   C. before 8:25 p.m.
B. after 8:30 p.m.   D. after 8:40 p.m.

----

22. Which car sustained damage to the front bumper?
A. FL. plate #4492GDX, red 2007 Honda
B. FL. plate #35434DE, red 2006 Ford
C. FL. plate #35434DE, black 2006 Ford
D. FL. plate #4492GDX, black 2007 Honda

----

23. What is the total number of persons involved in the accident?
A. 1   C. 3
B. 2   D. none of the above

----

24. The owner of the parked vehicle with damage to the rear bumper resides at:
A. 304 West Almeria Road, Banford
B. 183 Madison Street, Banford
C. 304 West Almeria Road, Sanford
D. 183 Madison Street, Sanford

----

25. Which of the following is correct?
A. The driver and owner of the red Honda is Tania Salters.
B. Ms. Wright's FL. driver's license identification number is W3547 28592 12323.
C. Officers Alberts and Sumpter completed a Vehicle Accident Report at 8:04 p.m.
D. Nancy Wright lives at 304 West Almeria Road, Sanford.

----

26. Which of the following is not correct?
A. The vehicle driven by Tania Salters had damage to the front bumper.
B. The vehicle driven and owned by Nancy Wright was a red 2009 Ford.
C. Tania Salters is 26 years old.
D. Ms. Salters' auto was a 2007 black Honda, FL. license plate 4492GDX.

Questions 27 - 34

27. An officer is reviewing a report she is preparing. It contains the following two rough drafts. Which of the two sentences are grammatically correct?

   1. The man who assaulted him, the cashier said, was about twenty years old and was wearing blue pants and a black, turtleneck sweater.

   2. The cashier stated that the male who assaulted him was about twenty years old and was wearing blue pants and a black, turtleneck sweater.

A. Only sentence 1 is grammatically correct.
B. Only sentence 2 is grammatically correct.
C. Both sentences 1 and 2 are grammatically correct.
D. Neither sentence 1 nor sentence 2 is grammatically correct.

----

28. An officer is asked by his partner to review a speech that the officer is preparing to give to new recruits. It contains the following two versions of one part of the speech. Which are grammatically correct?

    1. And other reasons why police should know the neighborhood is they can learn about drug dealers where they sell where they store their supply and other facts.

    2. Police should know drug dealers the neighborhood for the reason where they sell and hide their supply and other facts.

A. Only version 1 is grammatically correct.
B. Only version 2 is grammatically correct.
C. Both version 1 and 2 are grammatically correct.
D. Neither version 1 nor version 2 is grammatically correct.

----

29. An officer is preparing a report and has not decided which of two versions of a specific section he wishes to use. Which of the two versions are grammatically correct?

    1. The alleged burglar and his alleged accomplice has decided not to speak with the officer. Both stated that they will not cooperate in any manner.

    2. Both the alleged burglar and his alleged accomplice stated that they will not cooperate in any way and that they will not speak with the officer.

A. Only version 1 is grammatically correct.
B. Only version 2 is grammatically correct.
C. Both versions 1 and 2 are grammatically correct.
D. Neither version 1 nor version 2 is grammatically correct.

----

30. Police Officer Bruce Manow is preparing a speech that he will give to an elementary school class which his sergeant has asked him to visit. Which of the following two versions are grammatically correct?

    1. The police officer job is not easy to get. Police officer candidates must do well on a written test and then pass a number of other qualifying tests.

    2. The police officer job is not easy to get must do well on a written test and then pass a number of other qualifying tests.

A. 1 only is correct.

B. 2 only is correct.

C. Neither 1 nor 2 is correct.

D. Both 1 and 2 are correct.

----

31. Police Officer Susan Houston is preparing an instruction sheet on how to respond to oral inquiries. Which of the following two sentences are correct?

1. When responding to oral inquiries from the public, the police officer should keep in mind that the manner in which the response is given is as important as the accuracy of the response.

2. When a police officer responds to oral inquiries from the public, the police officer should keep in mind that the manner in which the response is given is as important as the accuracy of the response.

A. 1 only is correct.

B. 2 only is correct.

C. Neither 1 nor 2 is correct.

D. Both 1 and 2 are correct.

----

32. Police Officer James Valerios is checking the correctness of sentences in one of his reports. Which of the following two choices are correct?

1. Police Officers wear uniforms and are required to act professionally and be impartial. Because Police Officers are highly visible, the impression which Police Officers create is important in establishing in the public a sense of trust and fairness.

2. Police Officers wear uniforms and are required to act professionally and be impartial, because Police Officers are highly visible, the impression which Police Officers create is important in establishing in the public a sense of trust and fairness.

A. 1 only is correct.   C. Neither 1 nor 2 is correct.

B. 2 only is correct.   D. Both 1 and 2 are correct.

----

33. Officer Follins is asked to select the best summary (A, B, C, or D) of the following information: (The best summary is the one that expresses the information in the most clear, accurate and complete manner).

Place of accident: in front of 2625 North 77th Street, Seaside

Time of accident: 10:15 P.M.

Date of accident: October 12, 2016

Vehicle involved: 2007 Armada

Driver: Helen Kierston

Damage: cracked rear headlights and cracked rear bumper

Details: a metal garbage container rolled into the street and struck the 2007 Armada

-----

A. On October 12, 2016, at 10:15 a.m., in front of 2625 North 77th Street., Seaside, a metal garbage container rolled into the street and struck the 2007 Armada, driven by Helen Kierston.

B. On October 12, 2016, in front of 2625 North 77th Street., Seaside, a metal garbage container rolled into the street and struck the 2007 Armada, driven by Helen Kierston.

C. On October 12, 2016, at 10:15 p.m., in front of 2625 North 7th Street., Seaside, a metal garbage container rolled into the street and struck the 2007 Armada, driven by Helen Kierston.

D. On October 12, 2016, at 10:15 p.m., in front of 2625 North 77th Street., Seaside, a metal garbage container rolled into the street and struck the 2007 Armada, driven by Helen Kierston, causing cracked rear headlights and cracked rear bumper.

----

34. Police Officer Quinones obtains the following information at the scene of a traffic accident:

Date of accident: November 5, 2016

Time of accident: 3:15 P.M.

Place of accident: intersection of 7th Avenue and 67th Street, Largo

Vehicles involved: 2008 Nissan and 2006 Buick

Drivers: Benjamin Fogel (2008 Nissan) and Annette Traynor (2006 Buick)

Damage: dent on front passenger door of 2006 Buick

Police Officer Quinones drafts four versions to express the above information. Which of the following four versions is most clear, accurate and complete?

A. On November 2, 2016, at 3:15 P.M., at the intersection of 7th Avenue and

67th Street, Largo, a 2008 Nissan and a 2006 Buick were involved in a traffic accident. The 2006 Buick, owned by Annette Traynor, sustained a dent on the passenger's front door. The 2008 Nissan, driven by Benjamin Fogel, did not sustain any damage.

B. On November 5, 2016, at 3:15 P.M., at the intersection of 7th Avenue and 67th Avenue, Largo, a 2008 Nissan and a 2006 Buick were involved in a traffic accident. The 2006 Buick, owned by Annette Traynor, sustained a dent on the passenger's front door. The 2008 Nissan, driven by Benjamin Fogel, did not sustain any damage.

C. On November 5, 2016, at 3:12 P.M., at the intersection of 7th Avenue and 67th Street, Largo, a 2008 Nissan and a 2006 Buick were involved in a traffic accident. The 2006 Buick, driven by Annette Traynor, sustained a dent on the passenger's front door. The 2008 Nissan, driven by Benjamin Fogel, did not sustain any damage.

D. On November 5, 2016, at 3:15 P.M., at the intersection of 7th Avenue and 67th Street, Largo, a 2008 Nissan and a 2006 Buick were involved in a traffic accident. The 2006 Buick, driven by Annette Traynor, sustained a dent on the passenger's front door. The 2008 Nissan, driven by Benjamin Fogel, did not sustain any damage.

Questions 35 - 40

35. Police Officer Haas is informed by a female whose pocketbook was yanked from her hands while she was waiting for the bus that the perpetrator was a male with a red baseball cap, about five feet eleven inches tall and wearing a white T-shirt and dark pants.

Officer Haas looks down the street in an attempt to spot the perpetrator. According to the information provided by the victim, Police Officer Haas should: (Choose the best answer.)

A. question all males and females on the street.

B. question all males and females wearing a red baseball cap.

C. question all persons with the height of five feet ten inches to five feet twelve inches.

D. question all males on the street who are wearing a red baseball cap and are about five feet eleven inches tall.

----

36. Police Officer Gregorius notices that repulsive smelling fumes are emanating from a fire in a city garbage container at the corner of a crowded street. Police Officer Gregorius should:

A. immediately run into a nearby store and see if they have a fire extinguisher.

B. take off his shirt and throw it on the fire.

C. warn everyone to stay clear and contact the proper authorities.

D. wait for the fire to burn itself out before checking it out.

37. While on patrol, Police Officer Ben McDonnel discovers that a manhole cover in the middle of a busy street has been removed and pungent smoke is coming out of it.

Based on the preceding information, what is the first step that Police Officer McDonnel should take?

A. Call for backup since he is on patrol alone.

B. Quickly get all the persons and traffic away from the manhole and then notify the proper authorities.

C. Look for the manhole cover as it may be nearby.

D. Call the highway department and complain.

----

38. Your sergeant asks that you interview a Mr. Jeffrey Fredrich regarding a complaint received by his neighbor, Gail Sealy, that he is always leaving his dog unleashed and free to roam in Ms. Sealy's back yard. You have knowledge that there is a Mr. Jeffrey Fredrich, Sr. and a Mr. Jeffrey Fredrich, Jr. because they are the owners of a coffee shop where you are a customer. What is the first step you should take in this situation?

A. At the Fredrich home, interview both Jeffrey Fredrich, Sr. and Jeffrey Fredrich, Jr. as they have the same name.

B. Ask the sergeant for clarification of the name of the person to be interviewed.

C. Disregard the sergeant's instructions because you know both Mr. Fredrich. Sr. and Mr. Fredrich, Jr. and they are both fine people.

D. Do not ask questions of the sergeant, as he might get upset.

----

39. Police Officer Lorna Kelman is on patrol when a shop owner runs out of his store with his hands on his head, trying to stem a serious bleeding wound. The man yells out that he was robbed a minute ago and that the robbers sped away in a car.

Based on the preceding information, what should Police Officer Kelman do first?

A. Take the man back into the liquor store and question him regarding the robbery.

B. Interview all nearby persons to determine whether any of them witnessed the robbery.

C. Apply first aid to the shop owner to stop the bleeding and call for medical assistance and officer backup.

D. Officer Kelman should get in her patrol car and attempt to catch up to the robbers.

----

40. Prior to the start of your patrol, your sergeant gives the name and address of an elderly female who reported that she had been mugged and instructs you to interview her. From prior

experience, you know that this female is prone to hallucinations. What is the first step you should take?

A. Quickly carry out the instructions of the sergeant.

B. Don't interview the female, as this would be a waste of time.

C. Prepare a report that includes that the woman is prone to hallucinations and that because of that you prepared the report without interviewing her.

D. Check with her relatives to see if she has been hallucinating recently.

Questions 41 - 43

PL 70.05 MAXIMUM SENTENCE OF IMPRISONMENT FOR JUVENILE OFFENDER

TYPE OF CONVICTION	MAXIMUM TERM OF IMPRISONMENT
Type "A" felony (murder second degree)	life imprisonment
Type "A" felony (arson first degree or kidnapping first degree)	at least 12, but not more than 15 years
Type "B" felony	10 years
Type "C" felony	7 years
Type "D" felony	4 years

41. According to the preceding table, which of the following choices is a correct maximum term of imprisonment for conviction of the stated offense?

A. Murder in the second degree committed by a Juvenile Offender (maximum 15 years)

B. "C" felony committed by a Juvenile Offender (maximum 10 years)

C. "B" felony committed by a Juvenile Offender (at least 12 nor more than 15 years)

D. "C" felony committed by Juvenile Offender (7 years)

CPL 120.10 Warrant of arrest definition, function, form, and content

1. A warrant of arrest is issued by a local criminal court after the filing of an accusatory instrument for the purpose of arraignment. It directs a police officer or designated peace officers to arrest a defendant and bring him to court for arraignment.

2. It is signed by the issuing judge and must state the following:

　(a) name of issuing court,

(b) date of issuance of the warrant,

(c) name of offense(s) charged in the accusatory instrument,

(d) name of defendant to be arrested (or alias or description),

(e) police or peace officer(s) to whom warrant is addressed,

(f) direction that officer arrest defendant and bring him to court.

3. A warrant of arrest may be addressed to an individual police officer or classification of officers.

Multiple copies of a warrant may be issued.

-----

42. According to CPL 120.10, which of the following statements is correct?

A. A warrant of arrest must contain the date of the issuance of the warrant.

B. A warrant of arrest must have the signature of the D.A.

C. A warrant of arrest directs that the officer bring the defendant to the local penitentiary.

D. For privacy reasons, a warrant of arrest cannot contain the name of the defendant.

CPL 170.55 Adjournment in contemplation of dismissal (ACD)

After arraignment and before entry of plea of guilty or commencement of trial, the court MAY upon motion of the people or defendant, or upon its own motion and consent of both the people and the defendant, order an ACD (ADJOURNMENT IN CONTEMPLATION OF DISMISSAL).

The case is adjourned without a date. People may make an application to restore the case within 6 months. If that occurs, the court may restore it and proceed to trial. If the case is not restored, the accusatory instrument is deemed to have been dismissed in furtherance of justice at the end of the six-month period.

In case of a family offense, the ACD is for 1 year. The people may make an application to restore the case within 1 year.

The court can impose conditions (performance of public service, counseling, etc.) as part of an ACD.

An ACD is NOT a conviction or admission of guilt.

-----

43. According to CPL 170.55, which of the following statements is not correct?

A. An ACD is not an admission of guilt.

B. An ACD in a family offense proceeding is for one year.

C. When an ACD is ordered, the case is adjourned without a date.

D. The people must in all cases consent to the ordering of an ACD by the judge.

Question 44

Which of the following circles (A, B, C, D) matches the image of the "Dissected Circle?"

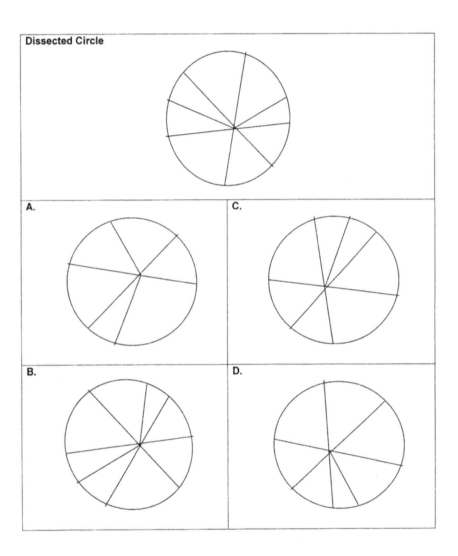

44. The drawing which best matches the image of the "Dissected Circle" is:

    A. Drawing A   B. Drawing B

    C. Drawing C   D. Drawing D

Deductive Reasoning Questions 45 - 47

Answer questions 45 - 47 based on the following extracts of two Criminal Procedure Law sections, CPL 120.70 and CPL 120.80.

CPL 120.70 A warrant of arrest issued by a district court, Miami criminal court or a superior court judge sitting as a local criminal court can be executed anywhere in the state.

A warrant of arrest issued by a city, town, or village court can be executed in the county of issuance or adjoining county (or anywhere in Florida upon the written endorsement of a local criminal court of the county in which arrest is to be made).

CPL 120.80 A warrant of arrest is executed any day of the week, any hour of the day or night.

The arresting police officer is not required to have the warrant in his possession at the time of making the arrest.

-----

45. Police Officer Marino, a Miami Police Officer assigned to a precinct in Miami, has in his possession a warrant of arrest issued by a district court for a person named Jack Wringer. Which of the following choices is correct?

A. Police Officer Marino cannot execute the warrant of arrest because it was issued by a district court and not a Miami court.

B. Jack Wringer cannot be arrested on that warrant if he is outside the county served by the district court.

C. Police Officer Marino may execute the warrant outside the state of Florida.

D. Police Officer Marino may execute the warrant because it was issued by a district court.

----

46. Police Officer Jane Goodwin, a Miami Police Officer assigned to a precinct in Miami, has in her possession a warrant of arrest issued by a town court in Cape Canaveral. Which of the following statements is correct?

A. Officer Goodwin can execute the warrant in Miami.

B. Officer Goodwin can execute the warrant only on weekdays in Miami.

C. Officer Goodwin can execute the warrant in Miami only if it has the written endorsement of a local criminal court of the county in which the arrest is to be made.

D. Officer Goodwin can execute the warrant in Louisiana.

47. According to CPL 120.70, which of the following is not correct?

A. A warrant of arrest issued by a superior court judge sitting as a local criminal court can be executed anywhere in the state.

B. A warrant of arrest issued by the Miami criminal court can be executed anywhere in the state.

C. A warrant of arrest issued by the board of a school district can be executed anywhere in the state.

D. Some warrants of arrest may be executed anywhere in the state.

"Because a thing is difficult for you to do, do not think that it is impossible for any man; but whatever is possible for any man to do and right for his nature, think that you can achieve it too."

- Marcus Aurelius

Questions 48 - 51 are based on the following map.

In answering the questions, follow the flow of traffic, as indicated by the arrows. Names of streets, buildings, public areas, and points 1-9 are indicated on the map.

48. Imagine that you are at Hargrove Avenue and Lincoln Street and then drive east to Franklin Avenue, then drive south to Elm St., then travel west to Ingersoll Avenue, you will be closest to which one of the following points?

A. 2   B. 4   C. 5   D. 9

49. If you start your drive at point number 7, then drive west to Ingersoll Avenue, then drive south to Dorance St., then east to Franklin Avenue, then drive south to Elm St., you will be closest to which one of the following points?

A. 1   B. 5   C. 6   D. 9

50. You are driving south in your patrol car and are at the intersection of Lincoln St. and Franklin Avenue. You are informed that an auto accident has just occurred at the intersection of Waring Street and Ingersoll Avenue. Assuming you must obey all traffic signs, which one of the following four choices describes the most direct route?

A. Drive south on Franklin Avenue to Fairfield St, then drive east on Fairfield St. to Ingersoll Avenue, then south to the intersection of Dorance Street and Ingersoll Avenue.

B. Drive south on Franklin Avenue to Fairfield St, then drive west on Fairfield St. to Ingersoll Avenue, then north to the intersection of Dorance Street and Ingersoll Avenue.

C. Drive north on Franklin Avenue to Fairfield St, then drive east on Fairfield St. to Ingersoll Avenue, then north to the intersection of Dorance Street and Ingersoll Avenue.

D. Drive south on Franklin Avenue to Fairfield St, then drive west on Fairfield St. to Ingersoll Avenue, then south to the intersection of Waring Street and Ingersoll Avenue.

----

51. You are driving north in your patrol car and are at Hargrove Avenue and E St. You are informed that a fight between two men is happening at the corner of Lincoln St. and Ingersoll Avenue. Which one of the following four choices describes the most direct route?

A. Drive south to Lincoln St. then west on Lincoln St. to the corner of Lincoln St. and Ingersoll Avenue.

B. Drive north to Lincoln St. then west on Lincoln St. to the corner of Lincoln St. and Ingersoll Avenue.

C. Drive south to Dorance St. then east on Dorance St. to Ingersoll Avenue, then north to Lincoln Street and Ingersoll Avenue.

D. Drive north to Lincoln St. then east on Lincoln St. to the corner of Lincoln St. and Ingersoll Avenue.

----

52. During the month of August 2016 there were 14 purse snatchings reported in Police Officer Devon's precinct. In five of the purse snatchings, the victims reported that the perpetrator was a white male, about 5 feet ten inches, shoulder length dark hair, "with a small, black star tattoo on the right side of his neck." All five victims reported that the man was carrying a large brown backpack. The five also reported that he had been wearing black dungarees and a black T-shirt.

During his patrol, Officer Devon stops four white males for questioning. He had recorded in his memo book the description given by the five witnesses. Which piece of information should Officer Devon consider the most important in identifying the suspected purse snatcher?

A. the black dungarees and black T-shirt

B. the shoulder length dark hair

C. the small, black star tattoo on his neck

D. the color of his skin

53. Prior to the start of his patrol, Officer Charles Briggs learns at the precinct that a female, about 75 years old, had been mugged one hour earlier by a person who the victim described as a "Hispanic, about twenty years old, with red hair tied in a shoulder length ponytail, and with a very crooked nose." She also described him as wearing black pants, a black T-shirt, and black sneakers.

During his patrol, Officer Briggs sees a group of four white or Hispanic males, about 20-25 years old, standing in front of Junior's Delicatessen. Officer Briggs stops his patrol car about twenty feet away to get a better look at the four males. Which of the following parts of the description provided by the victim is most important for Officer Briggs to consider in his attempt to identify the possible suspect?

A. the black T-shirt

B. the red hair tied in a shoulder length pony tail

C. the black sneakers

D. the crooked nose.

----

54. Police Officer Hanson is assigned to patrol an area which includes four public parks. During the prior four weeks, crime statistics show that four muggings were reported at the Jackson Park, all between the hours of 10:00 a.m. and 4:00 p.m. At the Washington Park six purse snatchings were reported. At the Bellmore Park eight strollers were stolen. At the Green Valley Park four bicycles were stolen. The muggings all occurred between 9:30 a.m. and 4:30 p.m. The purse snatchings occurred between 9:30 a.m. and 10:30 a.m. The strollers were stolen in the afternoon and before 3:00 p.m.

Officer Hanson works the 9:00 a.m. to 5:00 p.m. tour. On Monday, his sergeant instructs him to pay careful attention to stroller robberies. To try to reduce the number of stroller robberies, Office Hanson should patrol:

A. Washington Park

B. Green Valley Park

C. Bellmore Park

D. Green Valley Park and Washington Park

----

55. On Tuesday Officer Hanson works the 9:00 a.m. to 5:00 p.m. tour. His sergeant tells him that six bicycles have been stolen at the same park where four bicycles were stolen during the prior four weeks. To try to reduce the number of bicycles being stolen, Officer Hanson should patrol:

A. Washington Park

B. Green Valley Park

C. Bellmore Park

D. Columbus Park

Question 56 - 57

Answer questions 56 - 57 based on the following "Procedure for an Arrest on a Felony Offense."

Procedure for an Arrest on a Felony Offense

1. A person arrested for a felony offense must be handcuffed by the arresting officer.

2. The accused must be held in a police station or jail pending his or her ability to post bail in the amount set by the Judge at the first court appearance.

3. If the accused cannot post bail, the accused must be held in a secure facility.

4. If the accused posts bail, he or she must be released and ordered to appear at the next court date.

5. If the accused does not appear on the next scheduled court date, he or she forfeits any bail the Judge may have ordered and the Judge must order the issuance of an arrest warrant.

56. A person arrested on a felony charge appears before the Judge in court. The Judge sets a bail of $250,000.00. The person posts the entire bail and is released and ordered by the Judge to return on a specified date. On the return date, he does not appear. Based on the above "Procedure for an Arrest on a Felony Offense," which of the following statements is correct?

A. The person must be notified to appear on the next court date or a warrant of arrest will be issued.

B. The bail must be held on deposit by the court and returned to the person when he comes to court on the next court date.

C. If a warrant of arrest is ordered by the Judge, the bail is not forfeited.

D. The bail must be forfeited and a warrant of arrest must be ordered by the Judge.

57. According to the "Procedure for an Arrest on a Felony Offense," which of the following statements is correct?

A. If the accused refuses to post bail, he or she must be released and ordered to appear at the next court date.

B. The accused must be held in a police station or jail pending his or her ability to post bail in the amount set by the Police Captain.

C. A person arrested for a felony must not be handcuffed.

D. The Judge must order the issuance of an arrest warrant if the accused does not appear on the next scheduled court date.

"The secret of success is constancy of purpose."

- Bible

Questions 58 - 59

Answer questions 58 - 59 based on the following "Lost Property Procedure."

Lost Property Procedure

1. Any lost property in the possession of a Police Officer must be delivered by the officer to the "Lost Property Office" in the precinct by the end of the Officer's tour of the day.

2. The Lost Property Officer must inventory the property and safeguard it according to the requirements in the "Property Safeguarding Manual."

3. Property not claimed within 30 days shall be delivered by the Lost Property Officer to the "Central Lost Property Office" at One Police Plaza.

4. If the article is not claimed within one year following the delivery to the "Central Lost Property Office" at One Police Plaza, the article must be sold at auction pursuant to "Lost Property Auction Rules."

5. Funds collected at the auction, net of expenses, must be forwarded by the Central Lost Property Officer to the Miami Finance Administrator.

58. Officer Rolands receives a copy of the above "Lost Property Procedure" the same day in which a pedestrian hands him a diamond ring which he has found on the sidewalk. Officer Rolands used to work in a jewelry store and believes the ring to be costume jewelry. There is one hour remaining before Officer Roland's daily tour ends. Which of the following statements is correct procedure?

A. Officer Rolands should return the ring to the pedestrian and tell him it is costume jewelry.

B. Officer Rolands should take the ring to a jewelry store and have it examined before the end of his tour.

C. Officer Rolands should take the ring to the precinct's "Lost Property Office" before the end of his tour.

D. Officer Rolands should hold on to the ring for at least the following day and have it examined before wasting time delivering it to the "Lost Property Office."

59. After the passage of one year from the date property is delivered to the "Central Lost Property Office," the property:

A. must be returned to the precinct Lost Property Office.

B. must be forwarded to the office of the Miami Finance Administrator.

C. must be sold at auction pursuant to "Lost Property Auction Rules, 2016."

D. may be returned to the officer who found the property.

_____

Questions 60 – 68

60. You and another officer notice an elderly woman on the sidewalk. She tells you that a "tall man" just knocked her down and stole her pocketbook. You notice a "tall man" running down the block southbound to the end of the block where he makes a right turn. While your partner stays with the victim, you follow the man and observe him continuing to run for two blocks before making another right turn.

According to the information in the preceding passage, you would be most correct to radio that you last saw the man running:

A) north   B) south   C) east   D) west

----

61. While in your patrol car, you notice a car sideswipe a parked car and then continue northbound without stopping. You follow the car, which after four blocks makes a right turn and then after two more blocks makes a left turn.

According to the information in the preceding passage, you would be most correct to radio that you last saw the car heading:

A) north   B) south   C) east   D) west

----

62. A jewelry store employee runs out of a jewelry store, points down the block and shouts, "That guy just robbed me!" You shout for the man to stop, but he continues running westbound. After three blocks, he makes a left turn and runs for two more blocks before making another left turn.

According to the information in the preceding passage, you would be most correct to radio that you last saw the suspect heading:

A) north   B) south   C) east   D) west

----

63. You and another officer witness a purse being snatched from an elderly woman in front of the entrance to Ulmer Park. You shout for the man to stop, but he runs down the block in a westbound direction. You chase the man for three blocks before he turns left and then runs for another block, at which point he turns right.

According to the information in the preceding passage, you would be most correct to radio that the man was running:

A) north   B) south   C) east   D) west

----

64. While in your patrol car, you witness two men run out of a bar, each holding a pouch and a revolver. They quickly get into a car and head northbound. You follow. After three blocks, they make a right turn and then after two more blocks they make another right turn.

According to the information in the preceding passage, you would be most correct to radio that you last saw the car heading:

A) north   B) south   C) east   D) west

----

65. Your attention is drawn to a pedestrian shouting, "He took my bike!" and pointing to a man on a bike pedaling quickly on the sidewalk, away from the pedestrian and in a westbound direction. After three blocks, he makes a right turn and then after two more blocks he makes a left turn.

According to the information in the preceding passage, you would be most correct to radio that you last saw the man heading:

A) north   B) south   C) east   D) west

----

66. You and another officer notice a man in a wheelchair moaning on the sidewalk. He tells you that a "crazy looking man" just punched him on the head and then ran away. You notice a man running down the block northbound to the end of the block where he makes a left turn. While your partner stays with the victim, you follow the man and observe him continuing to run for three blocks before turning left.

According to the information in the preceding passage, you would be most correct to radio that you last saw the man running:

A) north   B) south   C) east   D) west

----

67. While in your patrol car, you notice a red car sideswipe a parked car and then drive off southbound without stopping. You follow the car, which after sixteen blocks makes a right turn and then after two more blocks makes another right turn.

According to the information in the preceding passage, you would be most correct to radio that you last saw the car heading:

A) east   B) south   C) north   D) west

----

68. A shoe store employee runs out of a shoe store, points down the block and shouts, "That guy just robbed the store!" You shout for the running man to stop, but he continues running northbound. After four blocks, he makes a left turn and runs for two more blocks before making a right turn.

According to the information in the preceding passage, you would be most correct to radio that you last saw the suspect heading:

A) north   B) south   C) east   D) west

"Let me tell you what has led me to my goal. My strength lies solely in my tenacity."

- Louis Pasteur

Question 69

Line
of
crates

A.

B.

C.

D.

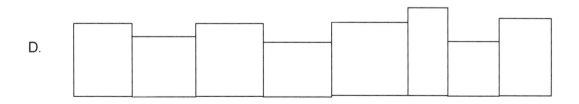

69. The above "Line of Crates" when viewed from the back would appear as which of the following choices?

A. Choice A   C. Choice C

B. Choice B   D. Choice D

Visualization Questions 70 - 75

Answer questions 70 - 75 based on the information contained in the following passage.

While on patrol, Police Officers Collins and Fogel are dispatched to 1673 Brittany Avenue, first floor "Archer Discount Store" at 9:45 p.m. on October 29, 2016. The owner of "Archer Discount Store" had just called 911 to report a burglary. They arrive at the store at 9:49 p.m. and are greeted by Mr. James Fontaine, the owner of the store and Mr. John Brighton, an employee of "Archer Discount Store."

Mr. Fontaine tells the officers that he and John Brighton had closed the store for the day at 8:00 p.m. They had locked the front and back doors and properly rolled down the security gate and padlocked it. Mr. Fontaine discovered the burglary at 9:30 p.m. when at home he happened to glance at the live video of his four security cameras. Although security camera #1 showed the outdoor front entrance and security camera #4 showed the outdoor back door area, it was with security cameras #2 and #3 that he saw the burglars. Security camera # 2 covered the outdoor roof skylight and security camera # 3 covered the inside area of the store, including the cashier area.

Two burglars, all dressed in dark blue and wearing black face masks, had broken the glass in the skylight and with a rope had lowered themselves into the store. The smaller of the two persons descended first and the much taller one followed. The person who descended first carried a black garbage bag and the other person held a flashlight in his right hand.

The two burglars took the $225.00 cash and coins that had been left in the cash register, an entire box of seven identical collectible statuettes worth a total of $1200.00, three expensive, identical watches worth a total of $900.00, two electric toasters worth $49.00 each, and six original signed watercolor paintings by a local artist worth $99.00 each. Mr. Fontaine tells the officers that he will prepare a complete list of missing items as soon as possible.

Mr. Fontaine tells Officer Fogel that he is 57 years old and lives at 3465 Baton Rouge Avenue in Brentwood. His cell number is 718-555-1283. John Brighton tells Officer Fogel that he is 27 years old and lives at 2835 West 125 Street, Brookville. His cell number is 781-555-2944.

Police Officers Collins and Fogel complete their investigation at 10:25 p.m. Before they completed their crime report, they performed a careful sweep of the store to make certain that the burglars had left.

-----

70. What was the most expensive individual item (one piece) stolen?

A. statuette

B. watch

C. watercolor painting

D. electric toaster

----

71. Which of the following statements is correct?

A. Mr. John Brighton, the owner of the store, is 57 years old.

B. Each of the burglars took $225.00 in cash and coins (total of $450.00).

C. Mr. John Brighton lives at 3465 Baton Rouge Avenue in Brentwood.

D. The total value of the watercolor paintings is $594.00.

72. Which one of the following statements is correct? Among the items stolen were:

A. six identical collectible statuettes worth a total of $1200.00.

B. two electric toasters worth a total of $49.00.

C. $450.00 cash and coins that had been left in the cash register.

D. three expensive, identical watches worth $300.00 each.

----

73. Which of the following statements is correct according to the information provided by Mr. Fontaine and Mr. Brighton?

A. Mr. Fontaine tells Officer Fogel that he is 57 years old and lives at 3645 Baton Rouge Avenue in Brentwood. His cell number is 718-555-1283

B. John Brighton tells Officer Fogel that he is 27 years old and lives at 2853 West 125 Street, Brookville. His cell number is 781-555-2944.

C. John Brighton tells Officer Fogel that he is 27 years old and lives at 2835 West 125 Street, Brentwood. His cell number is 781-555-2944.

D. Mr. Fontaine tells Officer Fogel that he is 57 years old and lives at 3465 Baton Rouge Avenue in Brentwood. His cell number is 718-555-1283.

----

74. Choose the best answer: The value of each of the statuettes that were stolen is closest to:

A. $171

B. $140

C. $150

D. $183

----

75. The total value of all items missing is:

A. $2,453

B. $3,617

C. $2,968

D. $3,017

Visualization Question 76

During his patrol, Police Officer Dawn Heller is called to the scene of an accident. The driver/owner of vehicle #3 stated that he was driving on Vine St. when car #1 hit his rear bumper, causing him to hit vehicle number 2.

Assume that all 3 vehicles were in their proper lanes of traffic.

Which of the following 4 diagrams best matches the statement of the driver of vehicle #3?

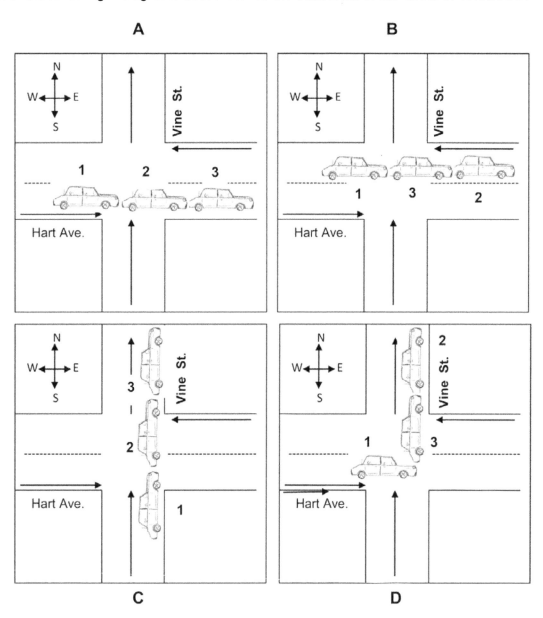

76. The diagram which best matches the statement of the driver of vehicle #3 is:

A. diagram "A"   C. diagram "C"

B. diagram "B"   D. diagram "D"

Questions 77 - 78

Answer questions 77 – 78 based on the following accident details.

Officer Nordstrum collects the following information at the scene of an auto accident:

Date of Accident: September 9, 2016

Time of accident: 4:15 p.m.

Place of accident: Intersection of Lavin Avenue and Reiker Avenue, Brookville

Driver: Barry Jones

Vehicle: 2008 Toyota Sienna

Damage: Vehicle struck a commercial metal garbage container protruding into the street.

-----

77. Officer Nordstrum is preparing a report of the accident and has four drafts of the report. He wishes to use the draft that expresses the information most clearly, accurately and completely. Which draft should he choose?

A. At 4:15 p.m., on September 9, 2016, at the intersection of Lavin Avenue and Reiker Avenue, Brookville, a vehicle driven by Barry Jones struck a commercial metal garbage container protruding into the street.

B. On September 9, 2016, at 4:15 p.m., at the intersection of Lavin Avenue and Reiker Avenue, Brookville, a 2008 Toyota Sienna driven by Barry Lones struck a commercial metal garbage container protruding into the street.

C. On September 9, 2016, at 4:25 p.m., at the intersection of Lavin Avenue and Reiker Avenue, Brookville, a 2008 Toyota Sienna driven by Barry Jones struck a commercial metal garbage container protruding into the street.

D. On September 9, 2016, at 4:15 p.m., at the intersection of Lavin Avenue and Reiker Avenue, Brookville, a 2008 Toyota Sienna driven by Barry Jones struck a commercial metal garbage container protruding into the street.

----

78. Officer Nordstrum is comparing the information he recorded in his memo pad (at the scene of the accident) to the information in his report. Which of the above choices (A, B, C, or D) has a detail that does not agree with the information in the officer's memo pad?

A. Date of Accident: September 9, 2016; Time of accident: 4:15 p.m.

B. Place of accident: Intersection of Lavin Avenue and Reiker Avenue, Brookville

C. Driver: Barry Jones: Vehicle: 2008 Toyota Sienna

D. Damage: Vehicle struck a commercial plastic garbage container protruding into the street

Answer questions 79 - 80 based on the following information gathered at a crime scene.

Officer Samuels responds to a car theft. She questions the owner of the vehicle who reported the car stolen and obtains the following information:

Suspect: Unidentified

Date of crime: August 25, 2016

Time of crime: between 7:20 p.m. and 11:40 p.m.

Crime: theft of car

Vehicle stolen: 2012 Volvo

Victim: owner of car, Frank Dolin

Place of crime: driveway in front of 247 18th Street, Miami

-----

79. Officer Samuels is preparing a report of the accident and has prepared four drafts of the report. She wishes to use the draft that expresses the information most clearly, accurately and completely. Which of the following drafts should she choose?

A. A car theft of a 2012 Volvo happened at the driveway in front of 247 18th Street, Miami, where Frank Dolin's car was parked for the night. The alleged thief is unidentified, as the theft happened in the evening hours.

B. On August 25, 2016, between 7:20 p.m. and 11:40 p.m., at the driveway in front of 247 18th Street, Miami, a 2012 Volvo owned by Frank Dolin was stolen by an unidentified suspect.

C. A car was stolen on August 25, 2016, between 7:20 p.m. and 11:40 p.m., at the driveway in front of 247 18th Street, Miami, owned by Frank Dolin. The suspect is unidentified.

D. On August 25, 2016, 247 18th Street, Miami, between 7:20 a.m. and 11:40 a.m., a 2012 Volvo owned by Frank Dolin was stolen by an unidentified suspect.

----

80. Officer Samuels is comparing the information he recorded in his memo pad (at the scene of the accident) to the information in his report. Which of the above choices (A, B, C, or D) has one detail that does not agree with the information in the officer's memo pad?

A. Date of crime: August 25, 2016; Time of crime: between 7:20 p.m. and 11:40 p.m.

B. Crime: theft of car; Vehicle stolen: 2012 Volvo

C. Victim: owner of car, Frank Dolin

D. Place of crime: driveway in front of 247 18th Avenue, Miami

----

Answer question 81 based on the following "Media Inquiry Procedure."

Media Inquiry Procedure

When a criminal case is pending in the courts, the Police Officer who made the arrest is prohibited from discussing the case with any newspaper, magazine, TV reporters and all other media. Exceptions to this are cases where:

1. a Florida court of competent jurisdiction formally orders the Police Officer to discuss one or more particulars of the case.

2. a Florida authorized Department orders such discussion.

3. the Police Officer is subpoenaed to testify by an authorized Florida or federal board.

In all cases, media inquiries made to the officer should be referred to HQ Media Services at One Police Plaza.

-----

81. Police Officer Jane Hollis arrests a drug suspect and confiscates two pounds of heroin. The suspect has been indicted and is in jail, waiting for trial. A newspaper reporter, Abigail Briggs, contacts Officer Jane Hollis and asks a quick question, the answer to which might help the reporter to investigate drug trafficking in the city. Officer Jane Hollis should:

A. Answer the question since it is a quick question.

B. Tell the reporter to contact her sergeant.

C. Answer the question only if the reporter is trustworthy.

D. Tell the reporter to contact HQ Media Services at One Police Plaza.

Inductive Reasoning Questions 82 - 83

Answer questions 82 - 83 based on the following highlights of "CPL 500.10: Definitions."

CPL 500.10: Definitions

SECURED BAIL BOND is a bond secured by:

    1) personal property greater than or equal to the undertaking, or

    2) real property at least 2 times the value of the undertaking (assessed value divided by equalization rate, or special assessing unit as defined in article 18 of real property tax law).

PARTIALLY SECURED BAIL BOND is a bond secured by a deposit of money not in excess of 10 per cent of the total amount of the undertaking.

UNSECURED BAIL BOND is a bail bond (other than an insurance company bail bond) that is not secured by any deposit or lien.

-----

82. Which of the following is an example of an unsecured bail bond?

A. a bail bond secured by a deposit of money not in excess of 10 per cent of the total amount of the undertaking

B. a bail bond secured by personal property greater than or equal to undertaking

C. a bail bond (other than an insurance company bail bond) that is not secured by any deposit or lien

D. a bond secured by real property at least 2 times the value of the undertaking

----

83. A bail bond secured by a deposit of money not in excess of 10 per cent of the total amount of the undertaking is a:

A. secured bail bond.

B. unsecured bail bond.

C. questionable secured bail bond.

D. partially secured bail bond.

----

84. Four witnesses to a hit and run accident tell Police Officer Valenti that they memorized the license plate number of the car that sped away from the accident. Which of the following license plate numbers is the most likely to be correct?

A. 8337AFR

B. 8587AFR

C. 8537AFR

D. 8531AFR

Answer question 85 based on the following table:

Summonses and Desk Appearance Tickets Issued by Police Officer Archer

Week	Dates	Parking Summonses	Moving Summonses	Desk Appearance Tickets
1	Nov. 1 – 7	14	15	4
2	Nov 8 -14	11	3	6
3	Nov 15 – 21	16	10	1
4	Nov 22 – 28	9	12	5
5	Nov 29 – Dec 5	14	10	7

85. Police Officer Archer is adding up the total number of all summonses and Desk Appearance Tickets issued by her during the above five-week period. Which of the following four formulas should she use to arrive at the correct number of summonses and Desk Appearance Tickets that she issued?

A. 14+10+7

B. 4+6+1+5+7

C. 14+11+16+9+14+15+3+10+12+10+4+6+1+5+7

D. 1(14+11+16+9+14) + 2(15+3+10+12+10) + 3(4+6+1+5+7)

----

86. Police Officer Harrison is informed by a person who has just been mugged on the sidewalk that the perpetrator was a male with a dark complexion, about five feet ten inches tall and wearing a yellow T-shirt.

Officer Harrison looks down the street in an attempt to spot the perpetrator. According to the information provided by the victim, Police Officer Harrison should:

A. question all males and females on the street.

B. question all females wearing a yellow T-shirt.

C. question all persons of about the height of five feet ten inches.

D. question all dark complexion males on the street who are wearing a yellow T-shirt and are about five feet ten inches tall.

----

87. Police Officer Mendez notices that a heavy tree branch has fallen on lane 3 and lane 4 of a busy, four-lane highway. He has several traffic cones with him. Police Officer Mendez should:

A. immediately barricade the four lanes to stop all traffic and thereby decrease the possibility of an accident.

B. immediately barricade three lanes with the cones and keep one lane open.

C. immediately barricade lanes three and four with the cones.

D. immediately barricade lanes one and two with the cones.

----

88. During her patrol, Police Officer Nancy Stewart notices that a heavy metal store sign approximately three feet wide and ten feet long has detached from the building and is now on the sidewalk. She has several traffic cones in her car.

Based on the preceding information, what is the first step that Police Nancy Stewart should take?

A. Call for backup since she is on patrol alone.

B. Place the cones around the sign to prevent injuries to passing pedestrians.

C. Block the traffic lane closest to the sidewalk.

D. Go inside the store and notify the store owner.

----

89. Your supervisor gives you five "Complaint Forms" with the following priority numbers:

3867   29643   0444   1783   8227

He asks you to organize the forms in ascending priority.

According to the above, the third Complaint Form would be Complaint Form number:

A. 1783   C. 8227

B. 29643   D. 3867

Answer questions 90 and 91 based on the following display of letters.

D	E	U	J	D	Y	M	Z	W	F	U	N	L
C	g	P	a	H	N	E	U	T	G	C	I	H
Z	K	Y	Q	G	E	C	P	V	F	E	Y	U
C	Y	N	U	S	R	L	Z	Q	F	N	M	J
H	J	W	Y	J	A	G	B	H	M	U	T	C
V	E	K	Z	E	Y	I	L	n	H	T	K	M
S	R	H	M	K	O	D	G	B	N	U	E	Z
A	G	V	U	M	Y	V	E	H	N	I	X	S
R	G	B	J	U	G	E	A	Z	B	N	U	Y
H	R	h	Y	E	K	X	D	V	W	Q	Z	N
U	K	F	T	M	B	E	Y	E	G	J	K	X
W	X	G	U	K	M	G	R	H	d	E	T	Y
X	S	R	Y	F	T	R	T	N	U	F	E	H

90. What is the total number of uppercase letter Hs that are in the above display?

A. 8

B. 9

C. 10

D. 11

----

91. What is the total number of uppercase letter Es that are in the above display?

A. 11

B. 12

C. 13

D. 14

----

92. Master sequence: Kæ9T17¥LµÆÆØH9MX//-\4ZTDt¥

A. Kæ9T7¥LµÆÆOH9MX//-\4ZTDt¥

B. Kæ9T7¥LµÆÆØH9MX/-\4ZTDt¥

C. Kæ9T17¥LµÆÆØH9MX//-\4ZTDt¥

D. Kæ9T7¥LµÆÆØH9MX//-\4ZTDt¥

----

93. Which of the following four choices matches exactly the following Master sequence of numbers, letters, and symbols?

Master sequence: X//-\\\4ZTD t¥$€ÆKR8B37¥LµÆÆt¥

A. X//-\\\4ZTD t¥$€ÆKR8B37¥LuÆÆt¥

B. X//-\\\4ZTD t¥$EÆKR8B37¥LµÆÆt¥

C. X//-\\\4ZTD t¥$€ÆKR8B37¥LµÆÆt¥

D. X//-\\\4ZTD t¥$€ÆRR8B37¥LµÆÆt¥

----

94. Which of the following four choices matches the "suspect license plate number?"
Suspect license plate number: 5269-0906*NM

A. 5296-0906*NM

B. 5269-0906*MN

C. 5269-0906*NM

D. 5269-0906*NM

----

95. Which of the following four choices matches the "suspect license plate number?"
Suspect license plate number: 9625-8371*RK

A. 9625-8317*RK

B. 9652-8371*RK

C. 6925-8371*RK

D. 9625-8371*RK

Answer question 96 and 97 based on the following table:

Summonses and Desk Appearance Tickets Issued by Police Officer Rinder

Week	Dates	Parking Summonses	Moving Summonses	Desk Appearance Tickets
1	June 1 – 7	24	11	4
2	June 8 - 14	21	8	7
3	June 15 – 21	26	12	2
4	June 22 – 28	19	9	6
5	June 29 – July 5	28	13	10

96. In which of the five weeks did Officer Rinder issue the greatest total number of summonses and tickets?

A. June 1 – 7
B. June 8 - 14
C. June 15 – 21
D. June 29 – July 5

----

97. What is the total number of Parking Summonses issued by Police Officer Rinder?
A. 39
B. 51
C. 118
D. 53

----

98. Four witnesses to a hit and run accident tell Police Officer Williams that they memorized the license plate of the car that sped away from the accident. Which of the following is the most like to be correct?

A. 7237SFG

B. 7587SFG

C. 7537SFG

D. 7531SFG

----

99. You and another officer notice an elderly man laying down on the street and bleeding from the head. He tells you that a tall man hit him with an umbrella. You notice the man running down the block northbound to the end of the block where he makes a right turn. While your partner stays with the victim, you follow the man and observe him continuing to run for two blocks before turning right.

According to the information in the preceding passage, you would be most correct to radio that you last saw the dog running:

A) north

B) south

C) east

D) west

----

100. While in your patrol car, you notice a car sideswipe a parked car and then drive off southbound without stopping. You follow the car, which after six blocks makes a right turn and then after two more blocks makes a left turn.

According to the information in the preceding passage, you would be most correct to radio that you last saw the car heading:

A) north

B) south

C) east

D) west

END OF PRACTICE TEST

PRACTICE TEST ANSWERS

Memory Answers

Study the photo below for the next ten minutes. Try to remember as many details about the people and objects as you can. During the ten minutes, you are not permitted to take any notes or write anything.

At the end of the ten minutes you will be asked to answer questions 1 – 10 (<u>without</u> looking back at the picture.)

(After ten minutes)

Instructions for questions 1 – 10:

<u>Without</u> looking back at the picture, answer questions 1 – 10 on the following page.

1. The number of protestors not wearing any type of mask is:

A. 0   B. 1   C. 2   D. 3

2. How many signboards are displayed in the picture?

A. 6   B. 7   **C. 8**   D. 9

3. How many people are wearing a white mask?

A. 2   **B. 3**   C. 4   D. 5

4. The capital letter that appears alone on one of the signs is:

A. "B"   B. "Z"   C. "R"   **D. none of the above**

5. The two protestors that are holding signs with "USA" and the crossed-out number "51" on them:

A. are both wearing black shirts.   C. are of the same height.

B. are both wearing white jackets.   D. are wearing black face masks.

6. The dark signboard that is ripped at the corner:

A. has the word "Peace" on it.

B. has the word "NO" on it.

C. has the letters "USA" on it.

D. none of the above (It is blank.)

7. How many signs have the letters "USA" on the sign?

A. 1   **B. 2**   C. 3   D. 4

8. The "smiley face":

A. is on a white background.

B. is being held above the heads of the crowd.

C. is on two signs.

D. does not have a nose.

9. How many signs have a "star" drawn on them?

A. 1   B. 2   C. 3   D. 4

10. How many signs do not have anything written, printed or displayed on them?

A. 0   **B. 1**   C 2   D. 3

Answers 11 - 15

Answer questions 11 - 15 based on the information contained in the following paragraphs.

Police Officers Frank Torres and Diane Washington were on patrol on August 13, 2016 when at **9:45 p.m.** they witnessed a minor traffic accident (at East 16th Street and Kings Highway in Miami). Officer Torres called the Police Dispatcher at 9:50 p.m. and reported that **the two drivers, and two passengers (one in each vehicle) did not sustain any personal injuries**. One of the vehicles, the one driven by a male named Felix Upton, did have minor damage to the windshield, and the other vehicle, driven by a male named Mark Levington, had extensive damage to the driver's side front door.

Officer Washington examined the driver's licenses, vehicle registration certificates and vehicle insurance identification cards. The auto driven by **Felix Upton, age 46, was a black 2012 Ford Edge, FL. license plate 4357ZB**, owned by the driver, residing at 1942 West 58th Street, Miami. Mr. Upton's FL. driver's license identification number is D274 43 662 and the expiration date is December 31, 2018.

The driver of the other auto was Mark Levington, age 52, residing at 2686 Manor Street, Miami. Mr. Levington's auto was a **blue 2011 Ford Escape, FL. license plate 607PHB**. Mr. Levington's driver's license identification number is A214 295 337 and the expiration is December 31, 2018.

Officers Torres and Washington completed a Vehicle Accident Report at 10:15 p.m. The report number was **48392747332**.

-----

11. What is the time of the accident?
A. 9:50 p.m.   **C. 9:45 p.m.**
B. 10:15 p.m.   D. before 9:30 a.m.
(The passage states, "…at 9:45 p.m. they witnessed a minor traffic accident.…")

----

12. How many persons were injured as a result of the traffic accident?
A. 1   C. 2
B. 0   D. none of the above
(The passage states, "…the two drivers, and two passengers (one in each vehicle) did not sustain any personal injuries.…")

----

13. Which car sustained extensive damage to the driver's side front door?
A. FL. plate #607PHB, black 2012 Ford Edge
B. FL. plate #4357ZN, black 2012 Ford Edge
C. FL. plate #4357ZN, blue 2011 Ford Escape
D. FL plate #607PHB, blue 2011 Ford Escape
(The passage states, "...vehicle driven by a male named Mark Levington, had extensive damage to the driver's door...Mr. Levington's auto was a blue 2011 Ford Escape, FL. license plate 607PHB.")

----

14. Which of the following statements is not correct?

A. The auto driven by Felix Upton, age 46, was a black 2012 Ford Edge.

B. The vehicle Accident Report number was 4839274732.
(The correct Accident Report number is 48392747332.)

C. Mark Levington, age 52, resides at 2686 Manor Street, Miami.

D. Mr. Upton's FL. driver's license identification number is D274 43 662.

----

15. Which of the following is correct?

A. The person residing at 1942 West 58th Street, Miami has a FL. driver's license identification number D274 43 665 with an expiration date of December 31, 2018.
(WRONG. The correct driver's license identification number D274 43 662.)

B. Mark Levington, age 25, resides at 2686 Manor Street, Miami.
(WRONG. "The driver of the other auto was Mark Levington, age 52....)

C. The auto driven by Felix Upton, is a black 2012 Ford Edge, FL. license plate 4357ZB.
(CORRECT. "The auto driven by Felix Upton, age 46, was a black 2012 Ford Edge, FL. license plate 4357ZB.)

D. The accident occurred at East 16th Street and Kings Highway in Marna.
(WRONG. "...they witnessed a minor traffic accident at East 16th Street and Kings Highway in Miami.)

Answers 16 - 20

Answer questions 16 - 20 based on the information contained in the following paragraphs.

Police Officers George Elton and Jasmine Colbert were on patrol in their squad car on September 17, 2016 when at **9:35 p.m.** a man approached them. The man pointed to his parked car, a silver Toyota, and stated that the red Ford Taurus parked behind it had just done some damage to the back of his car while the Taurus was parking. Police Officer George Elton called the police dispatcher at 9:40 p.m. and reported the traffic accident, which occurred in front of 924 6th Avenue, Palmetto. Police Officer Jasmine Colbert questioned the driver of the Taurus. Both Police Officers reported to the dispatcher that the driver of the silver Toyota and the driver of the damaged red Ford Taurus did not sustain any injuries. Also, there were no passengers in the two cars. One of the vehicles, **the silver Toyota, was driven and owned by a male, Fred Elkinson. It had moderate damage to the back bumper and rear tail lights**. The other vehicle, owned by a female, Barbara Baker, sustained no damage.

Officer Elton examined the driver's licenses, vehicle registration certificates and vehicle insurance identification cards. The auto driven by Fred Elkinson, age 51, was a 2008 silver Toyota, FL. license plate 36823EL, owned by the driver, residing at 62 West Garry Road, Palmetto. **Mr. Elkinson's FL. driver's license identification number is R3241 35532 32578** and the expiration date is October 31, 2018.

The owner of the Taurus was Barbara Baker, age 46, residing at 234 West 9th Street, Palmetto Ms. Baker's auto was a 2009 red Ford Taurus, FL. license plate KB3463H. Ms. Baker's driver's license identification number is D413 742 533 and the expiration is November 30, 2018.

Officers Elton and Colbert completed a Vehicle Accident Report at **9:50 p.m**. The report number was **224376654522.**

-----

16. Select the best answer: The time closest to the time of the accident is:
A. 9:35 a.m.   C. 9:40 p.m.
B. 6:50 p.m.   **D. 9:35 p.m.**
(**"D" is CORRECT.** "…when at 9:35 p.m. a man approached them. The man pointed to his parked car, a silver Toyota, and stated that the red Ford Taurus parked behind it had just done some damage to the back of his car while the Taurus was parking.")

----

17. Which car sustained damage to the rear bumper and rear tail lights?

A.   FL. plate #36823EL, red Ford Taurus

B.   FL. plate #3463HKB, silver 2008 Toyota

C.   FL. plate #36823EL, silver 2008 Toyota

("C" is CORRECT. One of the vehicles, the silver Toyota, was driven and owned by a male, Fred Elkinson. "The auto driven by Fred Elkinson, age 51, was a <u>2008 silver Toyota, FL. license plate 36823EL</u>...It had moderate damage to the back bumper and rear tail lights.")

D. FL. plate #3463HKB, red Ford Taurus

----

18. At what time was the Vehicle Accident Report completed?

A. 9:35 p.m.

B. 9:40 p.m.

C. 9:50 p.m.
("C" is CORRECT. "Officers Elton and Colbert completed a Vehicle Accident Report at <u>9:50 p.m.</u>")

D. 9:55 p.m.

----

19. Which of the following statements is correct?

A. The license plate number of the car owned by Barbara Baker is KD3463H.
(WRONG. Correct plate number is K<u>B</u>3463H)

B. The report number is 224376654522.
(CORRECT)

C. Police Officer Jasmine Colbert called the police dispatcher at 9:40 p.m.
(WRONG. <u>Officer Elton</u> called the dispatcher.)

D. The vehicle driven and owned by Fred Elkinson had moderate damage to the front bumper and rear tail lights.
(WRONG. Damage was to the <u>back</u> bumper and rear tail lights.)

----

20. Which of the following statements is correct?

A. Police Officer Jasmine Colbert questioned the driver of the Toyota.
(WRONG. Police Officer Jasmine Colbert questioned the driver of the <u>Taurus</u>)

B. Barbara Baker is 64 years old.
(WRONG. Correct age is <u>46</u> years old.)

C. Officers Elton and Colbert completed a Vehicle Accident Report at <u>9:05 p.m.</u>
(WRONG. Correct time is <u>9:50 p.m.</u>)

D. Mr. Fred Elkinson's FL. driver's license identification number is R3241 35532 32578. **(CORRECT)**

Answers 21 - 26

Answer questions 21 - 26 based on the information contained in the following paragraphs.

Police Officers David Alberts and Carol Sumpter were on patrol in their squad car on August 23, 2016 when at **8:25 p.m.** a female approached them. The female stated that she had just been involved in a car accident with the black Honda that was now stopped next to her car, a red Ford. Police Officer David Alberts called the police dispatcher at 8:33 p.m. and reported the traffic accident (which occurred in front of 1976 East 17th Street, Sanford). Police Officer Carol Sumpter questioned the driver of the black Honda. Both Police Officers reported to the dispatcher that both drivers did not sustain any injuries. **Also, there were no passengers in the two cars.** One of the vehicles, **the red Ford, was driven and owned by a female, Nancy Wright. It had damage to the rear bumper. The other vehicle, driven by a female, Tania Salters, had damage to the front bumper.**

Officer Alberts examined the driver's licenses, vehicle registration certificates and vehicle insurance cards. **The auto driven by Nancy Wright, age 38, was a red 2006 Ford, FL. license plate 35434DE, owned by the driver, residing at 304 West Almeria Road**, Sanford. Ms. Wright's FL. driver's license identification number is W3547 28592 12332 and the expiration date is September 30, 2018.

The driver and owner of the other auto was Tania Salters, age 26, residing at 183 Madison Street, Sanford, FL. Ms. Salters' auto was a 2007 black Honda, FL. license plate 4492GDX. Ms. Salters' driver's license identification number is H215 594 732 and the expiration is November 30, 2018.

Officers Alberts and Sumpter completed a Vehicle Accident Report at 8:40 p.m. The report number was 224376754321.

-----

21. Select the best answer. The closest time of the accident is approximately:

A. after 8:35 p.m.

B. after 8:30 p.m.

C. before 8:25 p.m.
(**"C" is CORRECT.** The officers learned of the accident at 8:25 p.m. Choices A, B, and D are all times after 8:25 p.m. and are therefore incorrect.)

D. after 8:40 p.m.

----

22. Which car sustained damage to the front bumper?

A. FL. plate #4492GDX, red 2007 Honda

B. FL. plate #35434DE, red 2006 Ford

C. FL. plate #35434DE, black 2006 Ford

D. FL. plate #4492GDX, black 2007 Honda
(Choice "D" has the correct details for the car driven by Tania Salters, the car which sustained the damage to the front bumper.)

----

23. What is the total number of persons involved in the accident?

A. 1

B. 2
("B" is CORRECT. "There were <u>no passengers</u> in the two cars." Therefore, the drivers were the only persons involved.)

C. 3

D. none of the above

----

24. The owner of the parked vehicle with damage to the rear bumper resides at:

A. 304 West Almeria Road, Banford

B. 183 Madison Street, Banford

C. 304 West Almeria Road, Sanford
(Choice "C" has the correct details for the car owned by Nancy Wright, the car which sustained the damage to the rear bumper.)

D. 183 Madison Street, Sanford

----

25. Which of the following is correct?

A. The driver and owner of the red Honda is Tania Salters.
(WRONG. Color of car is a <u>black</u> Honda.)

B. Ms. Wright's FL. driver's license identification number is W3547 28592 12323.
(WRONG. Correct number is W3547 28592 123<u>32</u>.)

C. Officers Alberts and Sumpter completed a Vehicle Accident Report at 8:04 p.m.
(**WRONG.** Correct time is <u>8:40</u> p.m.)

D. Nancy Wright lives at 304 West Almeria Road, Sanford.
(**"D" is CORRECT.** "The auto driven by Nancy Wright, age 38, was a red 2006 Ford, FL. license plate 35434DE, owned by the driver, <u>residing at 304 West Almeria Road, Sanford</u>....")

----

26. Which of the following is not correct?

A. The vehicle driven by Tania Salters had damage to the front bumper.

B. The vehicle driven and owned by Nancy Wright was a red 2009 Ford.
(**This statement is not correct.** The correct year of the Ford is <u>2006.</u>)

C. Tania Salters is 26 years old.

D. Ms. Salters' auto was a 2007 black Honda, FL. license plate 4492GDX.

Answers 27 - 34

27. An officer is reviewing a report she is preparing. It contains the following two rough drafts. Which of the two sentences are grammatically correct?

   1. The man who assaulted him, the cashier said, was about twenty years old and was wearing blue pants and a black, turtleneck sweater.

   2. The cashier stated that the male who assaulted him was about twenty years old and was wearing blue pants and a black, turtleneck sweater.

A. Only sentence 1 is grammatically correct.

B. Only sentence 2 is grammatically correct.

C. Both sentences 1 and 2 are grammatically correct.

D. Neither sentence 1 nor sentence 2 is grammatically correct.

28. An officer is asked by his partner to review a speech that the officer is preparing to give to new recruits. It contains the following two versions of one part of the speech. Which are grammatically correct?

1. And other reasons why police should know the neighborhood is they can learn about drug dealers where they sell where they store their supply and other facts.

2. Police should know drug dealers the neighborhood for the reason where they sell and store their supply and other facts.

A. Only version 1 is grammatically correct.

B. Only version 2 is grammatically correct.

C. Both versions 1 and 2 are grammatically correct.

D. Neither version 1 nor version 2 is grammatically correct.

(Version 1 starts with "And" – which is commonly frowned upon. It also needs commas, as in the following version:

Other reasons why police should know the neighborhood is that they can learn about drug dealers, where they sell, and where they store their supply.

Version 2 is a run-on sentence. Two or more sentences are joined without proper connecting words.)

----

29. An officer is preparing a report and has not decided which of two versions of a specific section he wishes to use. Which of the two versions are grammatically correct?

1. The alleged burglar and his alleged accomplice has decided not to speak with the officer. Both stated that they will not cooperate in any manner.

2. Both the alleged burglar and his alleged accomplice stated that they will not cooperate in any way and that they will not speak with the officer.

A. Only version 1 is grammatically correct.

B. Only version 2 is grammatically correct.
(In version 1 the subject of the sentence "alleged burglar and his alleged accomplice" (plural) disagrees with the verb "has" (singular)." A correct version would be:

The alleged burglar and his alleged accomplice <u>have</u> decided not to speak with the officer. Both stated that they will not cooperate in any manner.

C. Both versions 1 and 2 are grammatically correct.

D. Neither version 1 nor version 2 is grammatically correct.

30. Police Officer Bruce Manow is preparing a speech that he will give to an elementary school class which his sergeant has asked him to visit. Which of the following two versions are grammatically correct?

> 1. The police officer job is not easy to get. Police officer candidates must do well on a written test and then pass a number of other qualifying tests.

> 2. The police officer job is not easy to get must do well on a written test and then pass a number of other qualifying tests.

A. 1 only is correct.

(Version 2 is a run-on sentence. It needs to be expressed in two sentences.)

B. 2 only is correct.

C. Neither 1 nor 2 is correct.

D. Both 1 and 2 are correct.

----

31. Police Officer Susan Houston is preparing an instruction sheet on how to respond to oral inquiries. Which of the following two sentences are correct?

> 1. When responding to oral inquiries from the public, the police officer should keep in mind that the manner in which the response is given is as important as the accuracy of the response.

> 2. When a police officer responds to oral inquiries from the public, the police officer should keep in mind that the manner in which the response is given is as important as the accuracy of the response.

A. 1 only is correct.

B. 2 only is correct.

C. Neither 1 nor 2 is correct.

D. Both 1 and 2 are correct.

----

32. Police Officer James Valerios is checking the correctness of sentences in one of his reports. Which of the following two choices are correct?

1. Police Officers wear uniforms and are required to act professionally and be impartial. Because Police Officers are highly visible, the impression which Police Officers create is important in establishing in the public a sense of trust and fairness.

2. Police Officers wear uniforms and are required to act professionally and be impartial, because Police Officers are highly visible, the impression which Police Officers create is important in establishing in the public a sense of trust and fairness.

A. 1 only is correct.

(Sentence 2 is a run-on sentence. Two or more sentences are joined without proper connecting words.)

B. 2 only is correct.

C. Neither 1 nor 2 is correct.

D. Both 1 and 2 are correct.

----

33. Officer Follins is asked to select the best summary (A, B, C, or D) of the following information: (The best summary is the one that expresses the information in the most clear, accurate and complete manner).

Place of accident: in front of 2625 North 77th Street, Seaside
Time of accident: 10:15 P.M.
Date of accident: October 12, 2016
Vehicle involved: 2007 Armada
Driver: Helen Kierston
Damage: cracked rear headlights and cracked rear bumper
Details: a metal garbage container rolled into the street and struck the 2007 Armada

-----

A. On October 12, 2016, at <u>10:15 a.m.</u>, in front of 2625 North 77th Street., Seaside, a metal garbage container rolled into the street and struck the 2007 Armada, driven by Helen Kierston. **(WRONG. Correct time is 10:15 <u>P.M.</u>)**

B. On October 12, 2016, in front of 2625 North 77th Street., Seaside, a metal garbage container rolled into the street and struck the 2007 Armada, driven by Helen Kierston.

(WRONG. The time of the accident, "10:15 P.M.", is omitted.)

C. On October 12, 2016, at 10:15 p.m., in front of 2625 North 7<u>th</u> Street., Seaside, a metal garbage container rolled into the street and struck the 2007 Armada, driven by Helen Kierston. **(WRONG.** Correct address is 2625 North 7<u>7</u><u>th</u> Street., Seaside.)

D. On October 12, 2016, at 10:15 p.m., in front of 2625 North 77<u>th</u> Street., Seaside, a metal garbage container rolled into the street and struck the 2007 Armada, driven by Helen Kierston, causing cracked rear headlights and cracked rear bumper.

(CORRECT. Choice "D" includes all the information and has no factual errors.)

----

34. Police Officer Quinones obtains the following information at the scene of a traffic accident:

Date of accident: November 5, 2016

Time of accident: 3:15 P.M.

Place of accident: intersection of 7<u>th</u> Avenue and 67<u>th</u> Street, Largo

Vehicles involved: 2008 Nissan and 2006 Buick

Drivers: Benjamin Fogel (2008 Nissan) and Annette Traynor (2006 Buick)

Damage: dent on front passenger door of 2006 Buick

Police Officer Quinones drafts four versions to express the above information. Which of the following four versions is most clear, accurate and complete?

A. On November <u>2</u>, 2016, at 3:15 P.M., at the intersection of 7<u>th</u> Avenue and 67<u>th</u> Street, Largo, a 2008 Nissan and a 2006 Buick were involved in a traffic accident. The 2006 Buick, owned by Annette Traynor, sustained a dent on the passenger's front door. The 2008 Nissan, driven by Benjamin Fogel, did not sustain any damage.
(WRONG. Correct date is November <u>5</u>, 2016.)

B. On November 5, 2016, at 3:15 P.M., at the intersection of 7<u>th</u> Avenue and 67<u>th</u> <u>Avenue</u>, Largo, a 2008 Nissan and a 2006 Buick were involved in a traffic accident. The 2006 Buick, owned by Annette Traynor, sustained a dent on the passenger's front door. The 2008 Nissan, driven by Benjamin Fogel, did not sustain any damage.
(WRONG. 67th <u>Avenue</u> should be 67<u>th</u> <u>Street</u>. Also, vehicle is <u>driven</u> and not <u>owned</u> by Annette Traynor.)

C. On November 5, 2016, at <u>3:12 P.M.</u>, at the intersection of 7<u>th</u> Avenue and 67<u>th</u> Street, Largo, a 2008 Nissan and a 2006 Buick were involved in a traffic accident. The 2006 Buick, <u>driven</u> by Annette Traynor, sustained a dent on the passenger's front door. The 2008 Nissan, driven by Benjamin Fogel, did not sustain any damage.
(WRONG. Time should be <u>3:15</u> P.M.)

D. On November 5, 2016, at 3:15 P.M., at the intersection of 7th Avenue and 67th Street, Largo, a 2008 Nissan and a 2006 Buick were involved in a traffic accident. The 2006 Buick, driven by Annette Traynor, sustained a dent on the passenger's front door. The 2008 Nissan, driven by Benjamin Fogel, did not sustain any damage.

(**CORRECT.** Choice "D" includes all the information and has no factual errors.)

Answers 35 - 40

35. Police Officer Haas is informed by a female whose pocketbook was yanked from her hands while she was waiting for the bus that the perpetrator was a male with a red baseball cap, about five feet eleven inches tall and wearing a white T-shirt and dark pants.

Officer Haas looks down the street in an attempt to spot the perpetrator. According to the information provided by the victim, Police Officer Haas should: (Choose the best answer.)

A. question all males and females on the street.

B. question all males and females wearing a red baseball cap.

C. question all persons with the height of five feet ten inches to five feet twelve inches.

D. question all males on the street who are wearing a red baseball cap and are about five feet eleven inches tall.

("**D" is correct** because questioning all persons who fit just one of the description items is not logical. The combination of a red baseball cap, appropriate height, and the person being a male focuses on possible suspects without wasting time or involving other people.)

----

36. Police Officer Gregorius notices that repulsive smelling fumes are emanating from a fire in a city garbage container at the corner of a crowded street. Police Officer Gregorius should:

A. immediately run into a nearby store and see if they have a fire extinguisher.

B. take off his shirt and throw it on the fire.

C. warn everyone to stay clear and contact the proper authorities.

("**C" is correct** because the "repulsive smelling fumes" might be an indication of dangerous chemicals. This is a possible emergency situation. To protect the public, he should warn them to stay clear. Also, the proper authorities should be contacted so they can investigate the nature of the fumes and extinguish the fire.)

D. wait for the fire to burn itself out before checking it out.

----

37. While on patrol, Police Officer Ben McDonnel discovers that a manhole cover in the middle of a busy street has been removed and pungent smoke is coming out of it.

Based on the preceding information, what is the first step that Police Officer McDonnel should take?

A. Call for backup since he is on patrol alone.

B. Quickly get all the persons and traffic away from the manhole and then notify the proper authorities.

(**"B" is correct** because the "repulsive smelling fumes" might be an indication of hazardous chemicals. This is a possible emergency situation. To protect the public, he should warn them to stay clear. Also, the proper authorities should be contacted so they can investigate the toxicity of the fumes and extinguish the fire.)

C. Look for the manhole cover as it may be nearby.

D. Call the highway department and complain.

----

38. Your sergeant asks that you interview a Mr. Jeffrey Fredrich regarding a complaint received by his neighbor, Gail Sealy, that he is always leaving his dog unleashed and free to roam in Ms. Sealy's back yard. You have knowledge that there is a Mr. Jeffrey Fredrich, Sr. and a Mr. Jeffrey Fredrich, Jr. because they are the owners of a coffee shop where you are a customer. What is the first step you should take in this situation?

A. At the Fredrich home, interview both Jeffrey Fredrich, Sr. and Jeffrey Fredrich, Jr. as they have the same name.

B. Ask the sergeant for clarification of the name of the person to be interviewed.

 (**"B" is correct** because Police Officers should always get clarification when they have questions about instructions given to them by their supervisors. This helps the officer to properly carry out the instructions and helps to diminish unnecessary negative consequences that may result from misunderstood instructions.)

C. Disregard the sergeant's instructions because you know both Mr. Fredrich, Sr. and Mr. Fredrich, Jr. and they are both fine people.

D. Do not ask questions of the sergeant, as he might get upset.

----

39. Police Officer Lorna Kelman is on patrol when a shop owner runs out of his store with his hands on his head, trying to stem a serious bleeding wound. The man yells out that he was robbed a minute ago and that the robbers sped away in a car.

Based on the preceding information, what should Police Officer Kelman do first?

A. Take the man back into the liquor store and question him regarding the robbery.

B. Interview all nearby persons to determine whether any of them witnessed the robbery.

C. Apply first aid to the shop owner to stop the bleeding and call for medical assistance and officer backup.

(**"C" is correct** because immediate medical attention is required to stem the bleeding wound before the officer takes other action.)

D. Officer Kelman should get in her patrol car and attempt to catch up to the robbers.

----

40. Prior to the start of your patrol, your sergeant gives the name and address of an elderly female who reported that she had been mugged and instructs you to interview her. From prior experience, you know that this female is prone to hallucinations. What is the first step you should take?

A. Quickly carry out the instructions of the sergeant.

(**"A" is correct** because proper instructions should be carried out. If the officer has questions or suggestions, the officer should bring them to the attention of the sergeant and not modify or disregard them.)

B. Don't interview the female, as this would be a waste of time.

(WRONG. Proper instructions should be carried out.)

C. Prepare a report that includes that the woman is prone to hallucinations and that because of that you prepared the report without interviewing her.

(WRONG. By doing this, the instructions are not being carried out.)

D. Check with her relatives to see if she has been hallucinating recently.

(WRONG. The instructions should be carried out. Any proper investigation may be done after.)

Answers 41 - 43

PL 70.05 MAXIMUM SENTENCE OF IMPRISONMENT FOR JUVENILE OFFENDER

TYPE OF CONVICTION	MAXIMUM TERM OF IMPRISONMENT
Type "A" felony (murder second degree)	life imprisonment
Type "A" felony (arson first degree or kidnapping first degree)	at least 12, but not more than 15 years
Type "B" felony	10 years
Type "C" felony	7 years
Type "D" felony	4 years

41. According to the preceding table, which of the following choices is a correct maximum term of imprisonment for conviction of the stated offense?

A. Murder in the second degree committed by a Juvenile Offender (maximum 15 years)

(WRONG. Maximum is <u>life imprisonment</u>.)

B. "C" felony committed by a Juvenile Offender (maximum 10 years)

(WRONG. Maximum is <u>7 years</u>.)

C. "B" felony committed by a Juvenile Offender (at least 12 nor more than 15 years)

(WRONG. Maximum is <u>10 years</u>.)

D. "C" felony committed by Juvenile Offender (7 years)

(CORRECT. A "C" felony maximum term is <u>7 years</u>.)

CPL 120.10 Warrant of arrest definition, function, form, and content

1. A warrant of arrest is issued by a local criminal court after the filing of an accusatory instrument for the purpose of arraignment. It directs a police officer or designated peace officers to arrest a defendant and bring him to court for arraignment.

2. It is signed by the issuing judge and must state the following:

(a) name of issuing court,

(b) date of issuance of the warrant,

(c) name of offense(s) charged in the accusatory instrument,

(d) name of defendant to be arrested (or alias or description),

(e) police or peace officer(s) to whom warrant is addressed,

(f) direction that officer arrest defendant and bring him to court.

3. A warrant of arrest may be addressed to an individual police officer or classification of officers.

Multiple copies of a warrant may be issued.

-----

42. According to CPL 120.10, which of the following statements is correct?

A. A warrant of arrest must contain the date of the issuance of the warrant.

(CORRECT. "A warrant of arrest: 2. It is signed by the issuing judge and must state the following:

(a) name of issuing court,

(b) <u>date of issuance of the warrant</u>....)"

B. A warrant of arrest must have the signature of the D.A.

(WRONG. "It is signed by the <u>issuing judge</u>.")

C. A warrant of arrest directs that the officer bring the defendant to the local penitentiary.

(WRONG. A warrant of arrest directs the officer to bring the defendant to <u>court</u>.)

D. For privacy reasons, a warrant of arrest cannot contain the name of the defendant.

(WRONG. A warrant of arrest <u>can</u> contain the name of the defendant, or alias or description.)

CPL 170.55 Adjournment in contemplation of dismissal (ACD)

After arraignment and before entry of plea of guilty or commencement of trial, the court MAY upon motion of the people or defendant, or upon its own motion and consent of both the people and the defendant, order an ACD (ADJOURNMENT IN CONTEMPLATION OF DISMISSAL).

The case is adjourned without a date. People may make an application to restore the case within 6 months. If that occurs, the court may restore it and proceed to trial. If the case is not restored, the accusatory instrument is deemed to have been dismissed in furtherance of justice at the end of the six-month period.

In case of a family offense, the ACD is for 1 year. The people may make an application to restore the case within 1 year.

The court can impose conditions (performance of public service, counseling, etc.) as part of an ACD.

An ACD is NOT a conviction or admission of guilt.

-----

43. According to CPL 170.55, which of the following statements is not correct?

A. An ACD is not an admission of guilt.

B. An ACD in a family offense proceeding is for one year.

C. When an ACD is ordered, the case is adjourned without a date.

D. The people must in all cases consent to the ordering of an ACD by the judge.

(This statement is not correct because "After arraignment and before entry of plea of guilty or commencement of trial, court may upon motion of people or defendant, or upon its own motion and consent of both the people and the defendant, order an ACD.)

"The starting point of all achievement is desire."

– Napoleon Hill

Answer 44

Which of the following circles (A, B, C, D) matches the image of the "Dissected Circle?"

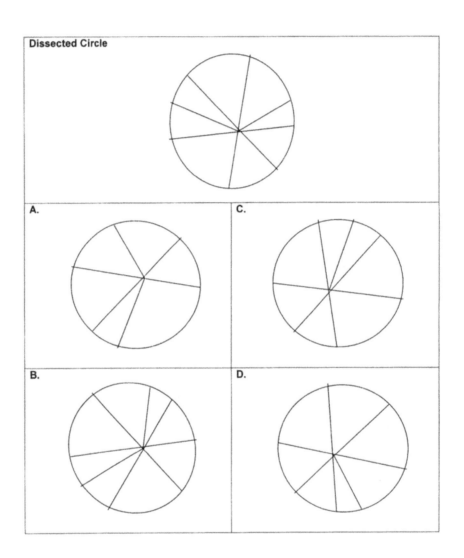

44. The drawing which best matches the image of the "Dissected Circle" is:

A. Drawing A (only 6 slices)   **B. Drawing B (identical 8 slices)**

C. Drawing C (only 7 slices)   D. Drawing D (only 7 slices)

Answers 45 - 47

Answer questions 45 - 47 based on the following extracts of two Criminal Procedure Law sections, CPL 120.70 and CPL 120.80.

CPL 120.70 A warrant of arrest issued by a district court, Miami criminal court or a superior court judge sitting as a local criminal court can be executed anywhere in the state.

A warrant of arrest issued by a city, town, or village court can be executed in the county of issuance or adjoining county (or anywhere in Florida upon the written endorsement of a local criminal court of the county in which arrest is to be made).

CPL 120.80 A warrant of arrest is executed any day of the week, any hour of the day or night.

The arresting police officer is not required to have the warrant in his possession at the time of making the arrest.

-----

45. Police Officer Marino, a Miami Police Officer assigned to a precinct in Miami, has in his possession a warrant of arrest issued by a district court for a person named Jack Wringer. Which of the following choices is correct?

A. Police Officer Marino cannot execute the warrant of arrest because it was issued by a district court and not a Miami court.

(WRONG. A warrant of arrest issued by a <u>district court</u> can be executed <u>anywhere in the state</u>.)

B. Jack Wringer cannot be arrested on that warrant if he is outside the county served by the district court.

(WRONG. A warrant of arrest issued by a <u>district court</u> can be executed <u>anywhere in the state</u>.)

C. Police Officer Marino may execute the warrant outside the state of Florida.

(WRONG. A warrant of arrest issued by a <u>district court</u>, Miami criminal court or a superior court judge sitting as a local criminal court can be executed <u>anywhere in the state</u>.)

D. Police Officer Marino may execute the warrant because it was issued by a district court.
(CORRECT. A warrant of arrest issued by <u>a district court</u>, Miami criminal court or a superior court judge sitting as a local criminal court can be executed <u>anywhere in the state</u>.)

46. Police Officer Jane Goodwin, a Miami Police Officer assigned to a precinct in Miami, has in her possession a warrant of arrest issued in Cape Canaveral. Which of the following statements is correct?

A. Officer Goodwin can execute the warrant in Miami.

B. Officer Goodwin can execute the warrant only on weekdays in Miami.

C. Officer Goodwin can execute the warrant in Miami only if it has the written endorsement of a local criminal court of the county in which the arrest is to be made.
(CORRECT. A warrant of arrest issued by a city, town, or village court can be executed in the county of issuance or adjoining county, <u>or anywhere in Florida upon the written endorsement of a local criminal court of the county in which arrest is to be made</u>).

D. Officer Goodwin can execute the warrant in Louisiana.

----

47. According to CPL 120.70, which of the following is not correct?

A. A warrant of arrest issued by a superior court judge sitting as a local criminal court can be executed anywhere in the state.

B. A warrant of arrest issued by the Miami criminal court can be executed anywhere in the state.

C. A warrant of arrest issued by the board of a school district can be executed anywhere in the state.
(CPL 120.70 does not address warrants of arrest issued by the board of a <u>school</u> district. Therefore, this statement is not correct.)

D. Some warrants of arrest may be executed anywhere in the state.

Answer 48

48. Imagine that you are at Hargrove Avenue and Lincoln Street and then drive east to Franklin Avenue, then drive south to Elm St., then travel west to Ingersoll Avenue, you will be closest to which one of the following points?

A. 2   B. 4   C. 5   **D. 9**

(For correct route, see dark arrows, above.)

Answer 49

49. If you start your drive at point number 7, then drive west to Ingersoll Avenue, then drive south to Dorance St., then east to Franklin Avenue, then drive south to Elm St., you will be closest to which one of the following points?

A. 1   B. 5   **C. 6**   D. 9

Answer 50

50. You are drining south in your patrol car and are at the intersection of Lincoln St. and Franklin Avenue. You are informed that an auto accident has just occurred at the intersection of Waring Street and Ingersoll Avenue. Assuming you must obey all traffic signs, which one of the following four choices describes the most direct route?

A. Drive south on Franklin Avenue to Fairfield St, then drive east on Fairfield St. to Ingersoll Avenue, then south to the intersection of Dorance Street and Ingersoll Avenue.

B. Drive south on Franklin Avenue to Fairfield St, then drive west on Fairfield St. to Ingersoll Avenue, then north to the intersection of Dorance Street and Ingersoll Avenue.

C. Drive north on Franklin Avenue to Fairfield St, then drive east on Fairfield St. to Ingersoll Avenue, then north to the intersection of Dorance Street and Ingersoll Avenue.

D. Drive south on Franklin Avenue to Fairfield St, then drive west on Fairfield St. to Ingersoll Avenue, then south to the intersection of Waring Street and Ingersoll Avenue.

Answer 51

51. You are driving north in your patrol car and are at Hargrove Avenue and E St. You are informed that a fight between two men is happening at the corner of Lincoln St. and Ingersoll Avenue. Which one of the following four choices describes the most direct route?

A. Drive south to Lincoln St. then west on Lincoln St. to the corner of Lincoln St. and Ingersoll Avenue.

B. Drive north to Lincoln St. then west on Lincoln St. to the corner of Lincoln St. and Ingersoll Avenue.

C. Drive south to Dorance St. then east on Dorance St. to Ingersoll Avenue, then north to Lincoln Street and Ingersoll Avenue.

D. Drive north to Lincoln St. then east on Lincoln St. to the corner of Lincoln St. and Ingersoll Avenue.

52. During the month of August 2016 there were 14 purse snatchings reported in Police Officer Devon's precinct. In five of the purse snatchings, the victims reported that the perpetrator was a white male, about 5 feet ten inches, shoulder length dark hair, "with a small, black star tattoo on the right side of his neck." All five victims reported that the man was carrying a large brown backpack. The five also reported that he had been wearing black dungarees and a black T-shirt.

During his patrol, Officer Devon stops four white males for questioning. He had recorded in his memo book the description given by the five witnesses. Which piece of information should Officer Devon consider the most important in identifying the suspected purse snatcher?

A. the black dungarees and black T-shirt

B. the shoulder length dark hair

C. the small, black star tattoo on his neck

(CORRECT. Unlike the items listed in choices "A," "B," and "D," this is the piece of the description that cannot be easily changed or disguised and that is also not too broad, like skin color.)

D. the color of his skin

----

53. Prior to the start of his patrol, Officer Charles Briggs learns at the precinct that a female, about 75 years old, had been mugged one hour earlier by a person who the victim described as a "Hispanic, about twenty years old, with red hair tied in a shoulder length ponytail, and with a very crooked nose." She also described him as wearing black pants, a black T-shirt, and black sneakers.

During his patrol, Officer Briggs sees a group of four white or Hispanic males, about 20-25 years old, standing in front of Junior's Delicatessen. Officer Briggs stops his patrol car about twenty feet away to get a better look at the four males. Which of the following parts of the description provided by the victim is most important for Officer Briggs to consider in his attempt to identify the possible suspect?

A. the black T-shirt

B. the red hair tied in a shoulder length pony tail

C. the black sneakers

D. the crooked nose.
(**CORRECT.** Unlike the items listed in choices "A," "B," and "C," this is the one piece of the description that cannot be easily changed or disguised.)

----

54. Police Officer Hanson is assigned to patrol an area which includes four public parks. During the prior four weeks, crime statistics show that four muggings were reported at the Jackson Park, all between the hours of 10:00 a.m. and 4:00 p.m. At the Washington Park six purse snatchings were reported. **At the Bellmore Park eight <u>strollers</u> were stolen. At the Green Valley Park four <u>bicycles</u> were stolen.** The muggings all occurred between 9:30 a.m. and 4:30 p.m. The purse snatchings occurred between 9:30 a.m. and 10:30 a.m. The strollers were stolen in the afternoon and before 3:00 p.m.

Officer Hanson works the 9:00 a.m. to 5:00 p.m. tour. On Monday, his sergeant instructs him to pay careful attention to stroller robberies. To try to reduce the number of stroller robberies, Office Hanson should patrol:

A. Washington Park

B. Green Valley Park

C. Bellmore Park
("At the Bellmore Park eight <u>strollers</u> were stolen" during the prior four weeks.)

D. Green Valley Park and Washington Park

----

55. On Tuesday Officer Hanson works the 9:00 a.m. to 5:00 p.m. tour. His sergeant tells him that six bicycles have been stolen at the same park where four bicycles were stolen during the prior four weeks. To try to reduce the number of bicycles being stolen, Officer Hanson should patrol:

A. Washington Park

B. Green Valley Park
("At the Green Valley Park four <u>bicycles</u> were stolen" during the prior four weeks.)

C. Bellmore Park

D. Columbus Park

Answers 56 - 57

Answer questions 56 - 57 based on the following "Procedure for an Arrest on a Felony Offense."

Procedure for an Arrest on a Felony Offense

1. A person arrested for a felony offense must be handcuffed by the arresting officer.

2. The accused must be held in a police station or jail pending his or her ability to post bail in the amount set by the Judge at the first court appearance.

3. If the accused cannot post bail, the accused must be held in a secure facility.

4. If the accused posts bail, he or she must be released and ordered to appear at the next court date.

5. If the accused does not appear on the next scheduled court date, he or she forfeits any bail the Judge may have ordered and the Judge must order the issuance of an arrest warrant.

56. A person arrested on a felony charge appears before the Judge in court. The Judge sets a bail of $250,000.00. The person posts the entire bail and is released and ordered by the Judge to return on a specified date. On the return date, he does not appear. Based on the above "Procedure for an Arrest on a Felony Offense," which of the following statements is correct?

A. The person must be notified to appear on the next court date or a warrant of arrest will be issued.

(**NOT CORRECT** because bail must be forfeited and the judge must order a warrant of arrest.)

B. The bail must be held on deposit by the court and returned to the person when he comes to court on the next court date.

(**NOT CORRECT** because bail must be forfeited now and the judge must order a warrant of arrest.)

C. If a warrant of arrest is ordered by the Judge, the bail is not forfeited.

(**NOT CORRECT**. Bail is forfeited.)

D. The bail must be forfeited and a warrant of arrest must be ordered by the Judge.

(**CORRECT.** "If the accused does not appear on the next scheduled court date, he or she forfeits any bail the Judge may have ordered and the Judge must order the issuance of an arrest warrant.")

----

57. According to the "Procedure for an Arrest on a Felony Offense," which of the following statements is correct?

A. If the accused refuses to post bail, he or she must be released and ordered to appear at the next court date.

(**NOT CORRECT**. Person must <u>not</u> be released if he does not post bail.)

B. The accused must be held in a police station or jail pending his or her ability to post bail in the amount set by the <u>Police Captain</u>.

(**NOT CORRECT**. Bail is set by the <u>judge</u>.)

C. A person arrested for a felony must not be handcuffed.

(**NOT CORRECT**. The person <u>must</u> be handcuffed.)

D. The Judge must order the issuance of an arrest warrant if the accused does not appear on the next scheduled court date.

(**CORRECT.** "If the accused does not appear on the next scheduled court date, he or she forfeits any bail the Judge may have ordered and the Judge must order the issuance of an arrest warrant.")

Answers 58 - 59

Answer questions 58 - 59 based on the following "Lost Property Procedure."

Lost Property Procedure

1. Any lost property in the possession of a Police Officer must be delivered by the officer to the "Lost Property Office" in the precinct by the end of the Officer's tour of the day.

2. The Lost Property Officer must inventory the property and safeguard it according to the requirements in the "Property Safeguarding Manual."

3. Property not claimed within 30 days shall be delivered by the Lost Property Officer to the "Central Lost Property Office" at One Police Plaza.

4. If the article is not claimed within one year following the delivery to the "Central Lost Property Office" at One Police Plaza, the article must be sold at auction pursuant to "Lost Property Auction Rules."

5. Funds collected at the auction, net of expenses, must be forwarded by the Central Lost Property Officer to the Miami Finance Administrator.

58. Officer Rolands receives a copy of the above "Lost Property Procedure" the same day in which a pedestrian hands him a diamond ring which he has found on the sidewalk. Officer Rolands used to work in a jewelry store and believes the ring to be costume jewelry. There is one hour remaining before Officer Roland's daily tour ends. Which of the following statements is correct procedure?

A. Officer Rolands should return the ring to the pedestrian and tell him it is costume jewelry. (**NOT CORRECT**. This is contrary to the Lost Property Procedure.)

B. Officer Rolands should take the ring to a jewelry store and have it examined before the end of his tour.
(**NOT CORRECT**. This is not one of the stated procedures.)

C. Officer Rolands should take the ring to the precinct's "Lost Property Office" before the end of his tour.

(CORRECT. Any lost property in the possession of a Police Officer must be delivered by the officer to the "Lost Property Office" in the precinct by the end of the Officer's tour of the day.)

D. Officer Rolands should hold on to the ring for at least the following day and have it examined before wasting time delivering it to the "Lost Property Office."

(NOT CORRECT. The ring must be delivered to the Lost Property Office before the end of the tour.)

----

59. After the passage of one year from the date property is delivered to the "Central Lost Property Office," the property:

A. must be returned to the precinct Lost Property Office.

B. must be forwarded to the office of the Miami Finance Administrator.

C. must be sold at auction pursuant to "Lost Property Auction Rules, 2016."

("C" is CORRECT. "4. If the article is not claimed within one year following the delivery to the "Central Lost Property Office" at One Police Plaza, the article must be sold at auction pursuant to "Lost Property Auction Rules, 2016." Choices A, B, and D are contrary to the procedure.)

D. may be returned to the officer who found the property.

_____

Answers 60 – 68

60. You and another officer notice an elderly woman on the sidewalk. She tells you that a "tall man" just knocked her down and stole her pocketbook. You notice a "tall man" running down the block southbound to the end of the block where he makes a right turn. While your partner stays with the victim, you follow the man and observe him continuing to run for two blocks before making another right turn.

According to the information in the preceding passage, you would be most correct to radio that you last saw the man running:

A) north

B) south

C) east

D) west

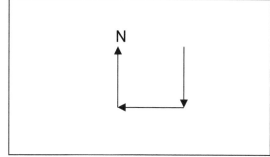

----

61. While in your patrol car, you notice a car sideswipe a parked car and then continue northbound without stopping. You follow the car, which after four blocks makes a right turn and then after two more blocks makes a left turn.

According to the information in the preceding passage, you would be most correct to radio that you last saw the car heading:

A) north

B) south

C) east

D) west

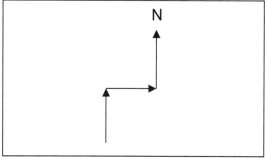

----

62. A jewelry store employee runs out of a jewelry store, points down the block and shouts, "That guy just robbed me!" You shout for the man to stop, but he continues running westbound. After three blocks, he makes a left turn and runs for two more blocks before making another left turn.

According to the information in the preceding passage, you would be most correct to radio that you last saw the suspect heading:

A) north

B) south

C) east

D) west

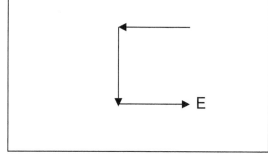

63. You and another officer witness a purse being snatched from an elderly woman in front of the entrance to Ulmer Park. You shout for the man to stop, but he runs down the block in a westbound direction. You chase the man for three blocks before he turns left and then runs for another block, at which point he turns right.

According to the information in the preceding passage, you would be most correct to radio that the man was running:

A) north

B) south

C) east

D) west

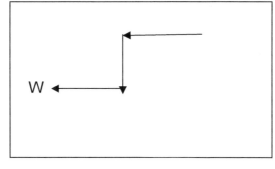

----

64. While in your patrol car, you witness two men run out of a bar, each holding a pouch and a revolver. They quickly get into a car and head northbound. You follow. After three blocks, they make a right turn and then after two more blocks they make another right turn.

According to the information in the preceding passage, you would be most correct to radio that you last saw the car heading:

A) north

B) south

C) east

D) west

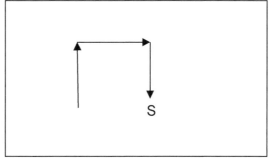

----

65. Your attention is drawn to a pedestrian shouting, "He took my bike!" and pointing to a man on a bike pedaling quickly on the sidewalk, away from the pedestrian and in a westbound direction. After three blocks, he makes a right turn and then after two more blocks he makes a left turn.

According to the information in the preceding passage, you would be most correct to radio that you last saw the man heading:

A) north

B) south

C) east

D) west

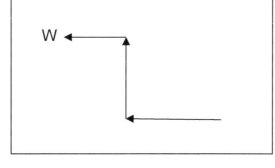

----

66. You and another officer notice a man in a wheelchair moaning on the sidewalk. He tells you that a "crazy looking man" just punched him on the head and then ran away. You notice a man running down the block northbound to the end of the block where he makes a left turn. While your partner stays with the victim, you follow the man and observe him continuing to run for three blocks before turning left.

According to the information in the preceding passage, you would be most correct to radio that you last saw the man running:

A) north

B) south

C) east

D) west

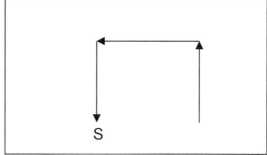

----

67. While in your patrol car, you notice a red car sideswipe a parked car and then drive off southbound without stopping. You follow the car, which after sixteen blocks makes a right turn and then after two more blocks makes another right turn.

According to the information in the preceding passage, you would be most correct to radio that you last saw the car heading:

A) east

B) south

C) north

D) west

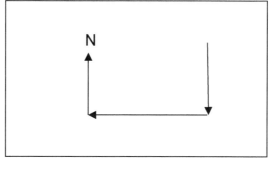

----

68. A shoe store employee runs out of a shoe store, points down the block and shouts, "That guy just robbed the store!" You shout for the running man to stop, but he continues running northbound. After four blocks, he makes a left turn and runs for two more blocks before making a right turn.

According to the information in the preceding passage, you would be most correct to radio that you last saw the suspect heading:

A) north

B) south

C) east

D) west

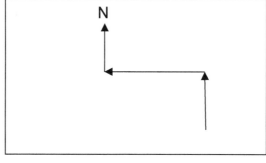

Answer 69

Line of crates

A.

B.

C.

D.

69. The above "Line of Crates" when viewed from the back would appear as which of the following choices?

A. Choice A   **C. Choice C**

B. Choice B   D. Choice D

The answer is "C." (To make the answer clear, we have filled-in each corresponding box with the same pattern.)

Visualization Answers 70 - 75

Answer questions 70 - 75 based on the information contained in the following passage.

While on patrol, Police Officers Collins and Fogel are dispatched to 1673 Brittany Avenue, first floor "Archer Discount Store" at 9:45 p.m. on October 29, 2016. The owner of "Archer Discount Store" had just called 911 to report a burglary. They arrive at the store at 9:49 p.m. and are greeted by Mr. James Fontaine, the owner of the store and Mr. John Brighton, an employee of "Archer Discount Store."

Mr. Fontaine tells the officers that he and John Brighton had closed the store for the day at 8:00 p.m. They had locked the front and back doors and properly rolled down the security gate and padlocked it. Mr. Fontaine discovered the burglary at 9:30 p.m. when at home he happened to glance at the live video of his four security cameras. Although security camera #1 showed the outdoor front entrance and security camera #4 showed the outdoor back door area, it was with security cameras #2 and #3 that he saw the burglars. Security camera # 2 covered the outdoor roof skylight and security camera # 3 covered the inside area of the store, including the cashier area.

Two burglars, all dressed in dark blue and wearing black face masks, had broken the glass in the skylight and with a rope had lowered themselves into the store. The smaller of the two persons descended first and the much taller one followed. The person who descended first carried a black garbage bag and the other person held a flashlight in his right hand.

The two burglars took the $225.00 cash and coins that had been left in the cash register, an entire box of seven identical collectible statuettes worth a total of $1200.00, three expensive, identical watches worth a total of $900.00, two electric toasters worth $49.00 each, and six original signed watercolor paintings by a local artist worth $99.00 each. Mr. Fontaine tells the officers that he will prepare a complete list of missing items as soon as possible.

Mr. Fontaine tells Officer Fogel that he is 57 years old and lives at 3465 Baton Rouge Avenue in Brentwood. His cell number is 718-555-1283. John Brighton tells Officer Fogel that he is 27 years old and lives at 2835 West 125 Street, Brookville. His cell number is 781-555-2944.

Police Officers Collins and Fogel complete their investigation at 10:25 p.m. Before they completed their crime report, they performed a careful sweep of the store to make certain that the burglars had left.

-----

70. What was the most expensive individual item (one piece) stolen?

A. statuette

(Each statuette is worth approximately $171 ($1200.00 divided by 7.)

B. watch
(THIS IS THE ANSWER. Each watch is worth $300.00 because 3 watches are worth $900.)

C. watercolor painting

(Each painting is worth $99.)

D. electric toaster

(Each toaster is worth $49.)

71. Which of the following statements is correct?

A. Mr. John Brighton, the owner of the store, is 57 years old.

(**WRONG**. Mr. <u>Fontaine</u> is 57 years old. Mr. <u>Brighton</u> is 27 years old.)

B. Each of the burglars took $225.00 in cash (total of $450.00).

(**WRONG**. <u>Total</u> cash and coins was <u>$225</u>.)

C. Mr. John Brighton lives at 3465 Baton Rouge Avenue in Brentwood.

(**WRONG**. Mr. <u>Fontaine</u> lives at this address.)

D. The total value of the watercolor paintings is $594.00.

(**CORRECT**. 6 watercolor paintings at $99 each = $594.)

----

72. Which one of the following statements is correct? Among the items stolen were:

A. six identical collectible statuettes worth a total of $1200.00

(**WRONG**. There were <u>seven</u> statuettes.)

B. two electric toasters worth a total of $49.00.

(**WRONG**. <u>Each</u> toaster is worth $49.)

C. $450.00 cash and coins that had been left in the cash register

(**WRONG**. Total cash and coins is <u>$225</u>.)

D. three expensive, identical watches worth $300.00 each.

(**CORRECT**. Paragraph 3: "three expensive watches worth a total of $900.00" – or <u>$300 each</u>.)

----

73. Which of the following statements is correct according to the information provided by Mr. Fontaine and Mr. Brighton?

A. Mr. Fontaine tells Officer Fogel that he is 57 years old and lives at <u>3645</u> Baton Rouge Avenue in Brentwood. His cell number is 718-555-1283

(**WRONG**. The correct street number is <u>3465</u>.)

B. John Brighton tells Officer Fogel that he is 27 years old and lives at <u>2853</u> West 125 Street, Brookville. His cell number is 781-555-2944.

(**WRONG.** The correct building number is <u>2835</u>.")

C. John Brighton tells Officer Fogel that he is 27 years old and lives at 2835 West 125 Street, <u>Brentwood</u>. His cell number is 781-555-2944.

(**WRONG.** John Brighton lives in <u>Brookville</u>.)

D. Mr. Fontaine tells Officer Fogel that he is 57 years old and lives at 3465 Baton Rouge Avenue in Brentwood. His cell number is 718-555-1283.

(**CORRECT.** All the information is correct.)

----

74. Choose the best answer: The value of each of the statuettes that were stolen is closest to:

A. $171

(**CORRECT.** This is the best "approximate" value. "…an entire box of seven identical collectible statuettes worth a total of $1200.00,": $1,200 divided by 7 = <u>$171.42</u>.)

B. $140

C. $150

D. $183

----

75. The total value of all items missing is:

A. $2,453

B. $3,617

C. $2,968

D. $3,017

Cash $	225
7 statuettes	1,200
3 watches for a total of	900
2 toaster, $49 each;	98
6 paintings, $99	594
Total	$ 3017

_____

Visualization Answer 76

During his patrol, Police Officer Dawn Heller is called to the scene of an accident. The driver/owner of vehicle #3 stated that he was driving on Vine St. when car #1 hit his rear bumper, causing him to hit vehicle number 2.

Assume that all 3 vehicles were in their proper lanes of traffic.

Which of the following 4 diagrams best matches the statement of the driver of vehicle #3?

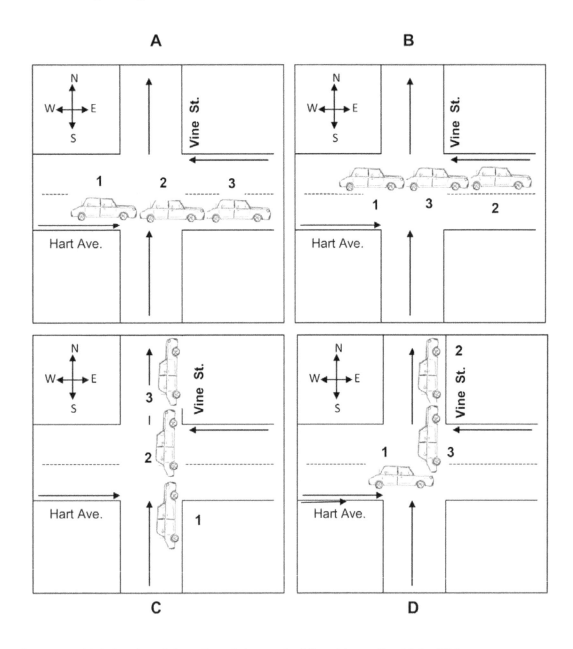

76. The diagram which best matches the statement of the driver of vehicle #3 is:

A. diagram "A"   C. diagram "C"

B. diagram "B"   **D. diagram "D"**

       (In proper lanes, "Car 1 hits car 3 which then hits car 2" is only displayed in Diagram "D.")

Answers 77 - 78

Answer questions 77 – 78 based on the following accident details.

Officer Nordstrum collects the following information at the scene of an auto accident:

Date of Accident: September 9, 2016

Time of accident: 4:15 p.m.

Place of accident: Intersection of Lavin Avenue and Reiker Avenue, Brookville

Driver: Barry Jones

Vehicle: 2008 Toyota Sienna

Damage: Vehicle struck a commercial metal garbage container protruding into the street.

-----

77. Officer Nordstrum is preparing a report of the accident and has four drafts of the report. He wishes to use the draft that expresses the information most clearly, accurately and completely. Which draft should he choose?

A. At 4:15 p.m., on September 9, 2016, at the intersection of Lavin Avenue and Reiker Avenue, Brookville, a vehicle driven by Barry Jones struck a commercial metal garbage container protruding into the street.

(WRONG. Type of vehicle, <u>a 2008 Toyota Sienna</u>, is not stated.)

B. On September 9, 2016, at 4:15 p.m., at the intersection of Lavin Avenue and Reiker Avenue, Brookville, a 2008 Toyota Sienna driven by Barry <u>Lones</u> struck a commercial metal garbage container protruding into the street.

(WRONG. Jones is misspelled <u>Lones</u>.)

C. On September 9, 2016, at <u>4:25 p.m.</u>, at the intersection of Lavin Avenue and Reiker Avenue, Brookville, a 2008 Toyota Sienna driven by Barry Jones struck a commercial metal garbage container protruding into the street.

(WRONG. Time is not correct. Time should be <u>4:15 p.m.</u>)

D. On September 9, 2016, at 4:15 p.m., at the intersection of Lavin Avenue and Reiker Avenue, Brookville, a 2008 Toyota Sienna driven by Barry Jones struck a commercial metal garbage container protruding into the street.

(BEST DRAFT. All the information is stated and is accurate.)

----

78. Officer Nordstrum is comparing the information he recorded in his memo pad (at the scene of the accident) to the information in his report. Which of the above choices (A, B, C, or D) has a detail that does not agree with the information in the officer's memo pad?

A. Date of Accident: September 9, 2016; Time of accident: 4:15 p.m.

B. Place of accident: Intersection of Lavin Avenue and Reiker Avenue, Brookville.

C. Driver: Barry Jones: Vehicle: 2008 Toyota Sienna

D. Damage: Vehicle struck a commercial plastic garbage container protruding into the street
(ONE DETAIL IS WRONG. The garbage container is <u>metal</u> and not <u>plastic</u>.)

Answer questions 79 - 80 based on the following information gathered at a crime scene.

Officer Samuels responds to a car theft. She questions the owner of the vehicle who reported the car stolen and obtains the following information:

Suspect: Unidentified

Date of crime: August 25, 2016

Time of crime: between 7:20 p.m. and 11:40 p.m.

Crime: theft of car

Vehicle stolen: 2012 Volvo

Victim: owner of car, Frank Dolin

Place of crime: driveway in front of 247 18th Street, Miami

-----

79. Officer Samuels is preparing a report of the accident and has prepared four drafts of the report. She wishes to use the draft that expresses the information most clearly, accurately and completely. Which of the following drafts should she choose?

A. A car theft of a 2012 Volvo happened at the driveway in front of 247 18th Street, Miami, where Frank Dolin's car was parked for the night. The alleged thief is unidentified, as the theft happened in the evening hours.
(WRONG. Date is missing. Time is missing. Language is sloppy.)

B. On August 25, 2016, between 7:20 p.m. and 11:40 p.m., at the driveway in front of 247 18th Street, Miami, a 2012 Volvo owned by Frank Dolin was stolen by an unidentified suspect.

(CORRECT. This is the best draft. It has all the information and is accurate.)

C. A car was stolen on August 25, 2016, between 7:20 p.m. and 11:40 p.m., at the driveway in front of 247 18th Street, Miami, owned by Frank Dolin. The suspect is unidentified. **(WRONG.** Type of car is not stated. Language is sloppy.)

D. On August 25, 2016, 247 18th Street, Miami, between 7:20 a.m. and 11:40 a.m., a 2012 Volvo owned by Frank Dolin was stolen by an unidentified suspect.

(WRONG. Time is not correct. It should be "between 7:20 p.m. and 11:40 p.m.)

----

80. Officer Samuels is comparing the information he recorded in his memo pad (at the scene of the accident) to the information in his report. Which of the above choices (A, B, C, or D) has one detail that does not agree with the information in the officer's memo pad?

A. Date of crime: August 25, 2016; Time of crime: between 7:20 p.m. and 11:40 p.m.

B. Crime: theft of car; Vehicle stolen: 2012 Volvo

C. Victim: owner of car, Frank Dolin

D. Place of crime: driveway in front of 247 18th Avenue, Miami
(The address should be "Street" and not "Avenue.")

Answer question 81 based on the following "Media Inquiry Procedure."

Media Inquiry Procedure

When a criminal case is pending in the courts, the Police Officer who made the arrest is prohibited from discussing the case with any newspaper, magazine, TV reporters and all other media. Exceptions to this are cases where:

1. a Florida court of competent jurisdiction formally orders the Police Officer to discuss one or more particulars of the case.

2. a Florida authorized Department orders such discussion

3. the Police Officer is subpoenaed to testify by an authorized Florida or federal board.

In all cases, media inquiries made to the officer should be referred to HQ Media Services at One Police Plaza.

-----

81. Police Officer Jane Hollis arrests a drug suspect and confiscates two pounds of heroin. The suspect has been indicted and is in jail, waiting for trial. A newspaper reporter, Abigail Briggs, contacts Officer Jane Hollis and asks a quick question, the answer to which might help the reporter to investigate drug trafficking in the city. Officer Jane Hollis should:

A. Answer the question since it is a quick question.

B. Tell the reporter to contact her sergeant.

C. Answer the question only if the reporter is trustworthy.

D. tell the reporter to contact HQ Media Services at One Police Plaza.

(CORRECT. Choices A, B, and C are contrary to the Media Inquiry Procedure.)

Inductive Reasoning Answers 82 - 83

Answer questions 82 - 83 based on the following highlights of "CPL 500.10: Definitions."

CPL 500.10: Definitions

SECURED BAIL BOND is a bond secured by:

1) personal property greater than or equal to the undertaking, or

2) real property at least 2 times the value of the undertaking (assessed value divided by equalization rate, or special assessing unit as defined in article 18 of real property tax law)

PARTIALLY SECURED BAIL BOND is a bond secured by a deposit of money not in excess of 10 per cent of the total amount of the undertaking.

UNSECURED BAIL BOND is a bail bond (other than an insurance company bail bond) that is not secured by any deposit or lien.

-----

82. Which of the following is an example of an unsecured bail bond?

FLORIDA LAW ENFORCEMENT BASIC ABILITIES TEST (BAT) EXAM GUIDE

A. a bail bond secured by a deposit of money not in excess of 10 per cent of the total amount of the undertaking

(**WRONG.** This is the definition of a <u>partially</u> secured bail bond.)

B. a bail bond secured by personal property greater than or equal to undertaking

(**WRONG.** This is the definition of a <u>secured</u> bail bond.)

C. a bail bond (other than an insurance company bail bond) that is not secured by any deposit or lien

(**CORRECT.** This is the definition of an <u>"Unsecured bail bond."</u>)

D. a bond secured by real property at least 2 times the value of the undertaking

(**WRONG.** This is the definition of a <u>secured</u> bail bond.)

----

83. A bail bond secured by a deposit of money not in excess of 10 per cent of the total amount of the undertaking is a:

A. secured bail bond.

B. unsecured bail bond.

C. questionable secured bail bond.

D. partially secured bail bond.

"PARTIALLY SECURED BAIL BOND is a bond secured by a deposit of money not in excess of 10 per cent of the total amount of the undertaking."

----

84. Four witnesses to a hit and run accident tell Police Officer Valenti that they memorized the license plate number of the car that sped away from the accident. Which of the following license plate numbers is the most likely to be correct?

A. 8337AFR

B. 8587AFR

C. 8537AFR

D. 8531AFR

Explanation:

The first digit "8" is the same in all choices.

Choice "A" differs from all other choices in that the second digit is "3" instead of "5." We can eliminate "A".

Choice "B" differs from the remaining choices by having an "8" as the third digit instead of "3." This leaves choices "C" and" D."

Choice "D" differs from the other choices in that the fourth digit is "1" instead of "7."

The correct choice is therefore **"C."**

Answer question 85 based on the following table.

___

Summonses and Desk Appearance Tickets Issued by Police Officer Archer

Week	Dates	Parking Summonses	Moving Summonses	Desk Appearance Tickets
1	Nov. 1 – 7	14	15	4
2	Nov 8 -14	11	3	6
3	Nov 15 – 21	16	10	1
4	Nov 22 – 28	9	12	5
5	Nov 29 – Dec 5	14	10	7

85. Police Officer Archer is adding up the total number of all summonses and Desk Appearance Tickets issued by her during the above five-week period. Which of the following four formulas should she use to arrive at the correct number of summonses and Desk Appearance Tickets that she issued?

A. 14+10+7

(**WRONG.** This totals only summonses and Desk Appearance Tickets issued Nov 29 – Dec 5.)

B. 4+6+1+5+7

(**WRONG.** This only totals the Desk Appearance Tickets issued.)

C. 14+11+16+9+14+15+3+10+12+10+4+6+1+5+7

(**CORRECT.** This gives us the total (137) of all summonses and Desk Appearance Tickets issued.)

D. 1(14+11+16+9+14) + 2(15+3+10+12+10) +3 (4+6+1+5+7)

(WRONG. This mathematical formula multiplies each parenthetical group of summonses issued by the number preceding the parenthesis and gives an incorrect total of 233 for the summonses and Desk Appearance Tickets issued.)

----

86. Police Officer Harrison is informed by a person who has just been mugged on the sidewalk that the perpetrator was a male with a dark complexion, about five feet ten inches tall and wearing a yellow T-shirt.

Officer Harrison looks down the street in an attempt to spot the perpetrator. According to the information provided by the victim, Police Officer Harrison should:

A. question all males and females on the street.

B. question all females wearing a yellow T-shirt.

C. question all persons of about the height of five feet ten inches.

D. question all dark complexion males on the street who are wearing a yellow T-shirt and are about five feet ten inches tall.

(D is correct because the description in "D" is the most specific of all the choices.)

----

87. Police Officer Mendez notices that a heavy tree branch has fallen on lane 3 and lane 4 of a busy, four-lane highway. He has several traffic cones with him. Police Officer Mendez should:

A. immediately barricade the four lanes to stop all traffic and thereby decrease the possibility of an accident.

B. immediately barricade three lanes with the cones and keep one lane open.

C. immediately barricade lanes three and four with the cones.

(Choice "C" is correct because lanes 3 and 4 are where the tree branch is laying and where car accidents might occur if the lanes are not blocked.)

D. immediately barricade lanes one and two with the cones.

----

88. During her patrol, Police Officer Nancy Stewart notices that a heavy metal store sign approximately three feet wide and ten feet long has detached from the building and is now on the sidewalk. She has several traffic cones in her car.

Based on the preceding information, what is the first step that Police Nancy Stewart should take?

A. Call for backup since she is on patrol alone.

B. Place the cones around the sign to prevent injuries to passing pedestrians.

(Choice "B" is correct because of all the choices, this is the **first** necessary thing that must be done to prevent possible injuries.)

C. Block the traffic lane closest to the sidewalk.

D. Go inside the store and notify the store owner.

----

89. Your supervisor gives you five "Complaint Forms" with the following priority numbers:

3867   29643   0444   1783   8227

He asks you to organize the forms in ascending priority.

According to the above, the third Complaint Form would be Complaint Form number:

A. 1783   C. 8227

B. 29643   **D. 3867**

(The order of priority in ascending order is: 0444, 1783, **3867**, 8227, 29643.

(For the following questions 90 and 91, see displays in the original questions.)

90. What is the total number of uppercase letter Hs that are in the above display?

A. 8

B. 9

C. 10

D. 11

91. What is the total number of uppercase letter Es that are in the above display?

A. 11

B. 12

C. 13

D. 14

----

92. Master sequence: Kæ9T17¥LµÆÆØH9MX//-\4ZTDt¥

A. Kæ9T7¥LµÆÆOH9MX//-\4ZTDt¥

B. Kæ9T7¥LµÆÆØH9MX/-\4ZTDt¥

C. Kæ9T17¥LµÆÆØH9MX//-\4ZTDt¥ (Correct answer)

D. Kæ9T7¥LµÆÆØH9MX//-\4ZTDt¥

----

93. Which of the following four choices matches exactly the following Master sequence of numbers, letters, and symbols?

Master sequence: X//-\\\4ZTD t¥$€ÆKR8B37¥LµÆÆt¥

A. X//-\\\4ZTD t¥$€ÆKR8B37¥LuÆÆt¥

B. X//-\\\4ZTD t¥$EÆKR8B37¥LµÆÆt¥

C. X//-\\\4ZTD t¥$€ÆKR8B37¥LµÆÆt¥ (Correct Answer)

D. X//-\\\4ZTD t¥$€ÆRR8B37¥LµÆÆt¥

----

94. Which of the following four choices matches the "suspect license plate number?"

Suspect license plate number: 5269-0906*NM

A. 5296-0906*NM

B. 5269-0906*MN

C. 5269-0906*NM

D. 5269-0906*NM (Correct answer)

----

95. Which of the following four choices matches the "suspect license plate number?"

Suspect license plate number: 9625-8371*RK

A. 9625-8317*RK

B. 9652-8371*RK

C. 6925-8371*RK

D. 9625-8371*RK (Correct answer)

Answer question 96 and 97 based on the following table:

Summonses and Desk Appearance Tickets Issued by Police Officer Rinder

Week	Dates	Parking Summonses	Moving Summonses	Desk Appearance Tickets
1	June 1 – 7	24	11	4
2	June 8 - 14	21	8	7
3	June 15 – 21	26	12	2
4	June 22 – 28	19	9	6
5	June 29 – July 5	28	13	10

96. In which of the five weeks did Officer Rinder issue the greatest total number of summonses and tickets?

A. June 1 – 7
B. June 8 - 14
C. June 15 – 21
D. June 29 – July 5 (28 + 13 + 10 = 51)

----

97. What is the total number of Parking Summonses issued by Police Officer Rinder?
A. 39
B. 51
C. 118 (24 + 21 + 26 + 19 + 28)
D. 53

----

98. Four witnesses to a hit and run accident tell Police Officer Williams that they memorized the license plate of the car that sped away from the accident. Which of the following is the most like to be correct?

A. 7237SFG

B. 7587SFG

C. 7537SFG

(Choice "C" is the most likely to be correct. This is the plate number whose numerals agree with most other plate numbers.)

D. 7531SFG

----

99. You and another officer notice an elderly man laying down on the street and bleeding from the head. He tells you that a tall man hit him with an umbrella. You notice the man running down the block northbound to the end of the block where he makes a right turn. While your partner stays with the victim, you follow the man and observe him continuing to run for two blocks before turning right.

According to the information in the preceding passage, you would be most correct to radio that you last saw the dog running:

A) north   **B) south**   C) east   D) west

----

100. While in your patrol car, you notice a car sideswipe a parked car and then drive off southbound without stopping. You follow the car, which after six blocks makes a right turn and then after two more blocks makes a left turn.

According to the information in the preceding passage, you would be most correct to radio that you last saw the car heading:

A) north   **B) south**   C) east   D) west

END OF PRACTICE TEST

ANSWER KEY- PRACTICE TEST

1. A	26. B	51. D	76. D
2. C	27. C	52. C	77. D
3. B	28. D	53. D	78. D
4. D	29. B	54. C	79. B
5. A	30. A	55. B	80. D
6. D	31. D	56. D	81. D
7. B	32. A	57. D	82. C
8. D	33. D	58. C	83. D
9. A	34. D	59. C	84. C
10. B	35. D	60. A	85. C
11. C	36. C	61. A	86. D
12. B	37. B	62. C	87. C
13. D	38. B	63. D	88. B
14. B	39. C	64. B	89. D
15. C	40. A	65. D	90. C
16. D	41. D	66. B	91. D
17. C	42. A	67. C	92. C
18. C	43. D	68. A	93. C
19. B	44. B	69. C	94. D
20. D	45. D	70. B	95. D
21. C	46. C	71. D	96. D
22. D	47. C	72. D	97. C
23. B	48. D	73. D	98. C
24. C	49. C	74. A	99. B
25. D	50. D	75. D	100. B

TEST-TAKING SUGGESTIONS

1. Get a good night's sleep! The night before the exam is not the time to go to a party or to a sports game. Scientific studies have shown that sleep deprivation dulls the mind.

2. If possible, try not to cram. If you can, review the exercises, suggestions and hints, and practice tests. If you have been studying correctly, you owe it to yourself to rest. Cramming often hurts instead of helping. Pace yourself each day and you won't feel the need to sprint at the last moment.

3. Pay careful attention to the time and location of the test site. Plan to get there early, in comfort and without having to rush. For more than thirty years I have heard many horror stories of candidates not arriving at the test site on time.

4. Do <u>not</u> go into the test hungry. Eat and drink enough to last you through the test. Keep hydrated.

5. At the test site, listen attentively and don't take anything for granted. Follow directions carefully. Make sure that you don't miss any information that might help you get a higher score.

6. If you have time, familiarize yourself with the computer you will be using. Check to see if it is working properly. If there are any problems, bring them to the attention of the proctor as soon as possible.

7. Crystallize in your mind how many questions you must answer - and the types of questions.

8. Quickly develop a time budget - and during the exam check the time <u>on your watch</u> to make sure you are not falling behind. Do not rely on the proctor to keep you informed of the time. Remember that you are not allowed to use a cell phone.

9. Usually every question is worth the same as the other questions. Don't spend too much time on any one question (unless you have finished all the other questions and are satisfied with your answers).

10. Read each question carefully. Select the best choice – and try to figure out why each of the other choices is not correct.

11. If you find during the test that there are questions for which you believe there is more than one valid answer, do not lose time thinking about it. Select the best answer that you can - and go on.

12. If during the test you feel tense or too nervous, try to stretch your body to relieve the uncomfortable symptoms. If you need to, take a minute to breathe in and out.

13. Don't pay any attention to people leaving before you. Chances are they will not do as well as you.

<u>GOOD LUCK !!!</u>

_____

Other Civil Service Jobs for Which We Have Exam Prep Books

JOB	Title of Exam Prep Book
New York State Unified Court System	
Court Office Assistant	Court Office Assistant
Senior Court Office Assistant	Court Office Assistant
Court Assistant	Court Office Assistant
New York City	
Police Officer	Police Officer Exam New York City
Police Officer	Police Officer New York City Speed-Prep
Sanitation Worker	Sanitation Worker Exam New York City
Sanitation Worker	Sanitation Worker Exam New York City Speed-Prep
Bridge and Tunnel Police Officer	Bridge and Tunnel Officer Exam New York City
Traffic Enforcement Agent (NYC)	Traffic Enforcement Agent New York City
School Safety Agent (NYC)	School Safety Agent New York City
Florida	
Law Enforcement	Florida Law Enforcement Basic Abilities Test (BAT) Exam Guide
National	
Postal Test	Pass the New Postal Test 473E Second Edition
Postal Test	Postal Test 473E - Speed Study Guide

Books by Angelo Tropea
Non-Fiction

Florida Law Enforcement Basic Abilities Test (BAT) Exam Guide

School Safety Agent New York City

Police Officer Exam New York City
Police Officer Exam New York City Speed-Prep

Sanitation Worker Exam New York City
Sanitation Worker New York City Speed-Study Guide

Bridge and Tunnel Officer Exam New York City

Traffic Enforcement Agent

Court Office Assistant

Pass the New York Notary Public Exam
Pass the New York Notary Public Exam (Questions and Answers)
Notary Public Journal of Notarial Acts
Notary Public Journal 600 Entries
Notary Public Journal Large Entries
Notary Public Journal Two-Page Entries
New York Notary Public Exam Speed-Study Guide
New York Notary Public Reference Guide

California Notary Public Exam

Pass the New Postal Test 2010 Edition
Pass the New Postal Test Second Edition
Postal Test 473E Study Guide

Pass the New Citizenship Test 2012 Edition
Pass the New Citizenship Test Third Edition
Pass the New Citizenship Test Questions and Answers (English, Spanish and Chinese Editions)

Examen de Ciudadania Americana Español Y Inglés

Pass the New Citizenship Test Quick Civics Lessons
Quick Civics Lessons from USICS and Civics Cards for Cut-Out

Canadian Citizenship Test

Goldmine of Baby Names Boys and Girls
Goldmine of Baby Names Boys
Goldmine of Baby Names Girls

Aliens and UFOs: Case Closed
Zombie Pocket Guide

Cruise Fan Tips and Tricks How to Get the Most Out of Your Cruise Adventure
Cruise Fan Cruising With Norwegian
Cruise Fan Bermuda Cruise

NYS Surrogate's Court Procedure Act Vol. 1
NYS Surrogate's Court Procedure Act Vol. 2
NYS Surrogate's Court Procedure Act Vol. 3
NYS Surrogate's Court Procedure Act Vol. 4

Amazing Science News and Facts No. 1

Arizona Civics Test
North Dakota Civics Test
Utah Civics Test
Idaho Civics Test

Fiction
Pinocchio and the Dragons of Martoon (age 12 and up)

<u>NOTES</u>

NOTES

NOTES